Dinner Just for Two

Dinner Just for Two

Christina Lane

THE COUNTRYMAN PRESS
A division of W. W. Norton & Company
Independent Publishers Since 1923

For information about permission to reproduce selections from this book, write to
Permissions, The Countryman Press, 500 Fifth Avenue, New York, NY 10110

For information about special discounts for bulk purchases, please contact
W. W. Norton Special Sales at specialsales@wwnorton.com or 800-233-4830

Manufacturing through Asia Pacific Offset
Book design by Anna Reich
Production manager: Devon Zahn

Library of Congress Cataloging-in-Publication Data

Names: Lane, Christina, 1984-
Title: Dinner just for two / Christina Lane.
Description: New York, NY : Countryman Press, a division of W. W. Norton &
Company Independent Publishers Since 1923, [2019] | Includes index.
Identifiers: LCCN 2018048585 | ISBN 9781682680094 (hardcover)
Subjects: LCSH: Cooking for two. | LCGFT: Cookbooks.
Classification: LCC TX652 .L24593 2019 | DDC 641.5/612—dc23
LC record available at https://lccn.loc.gov/2018048585

The Countryman Press
www.countrymanpress.com

A division of W. W. Norton & Company, Inc.
500 Fifth Avenue, New York, NY 10110
www.wwnorton.com

1 0 9 8 7 6 5 4 3 2 1

To Brian. For everything.

This unexpected career has put me on a whirlwind path—you
always set me straight and steer me toward the big picture.
If no one hears our small-batch cooking gospel, at least you
believed in me. It means the world to me. I love you.

And to Camille, my sweet baby. Your face is the reason I get out
of bed in the morning, and I work hard every day to show you
how to chase your own dreams someday. Mama loves you.

CONTENTS

CHAPTER 3. SMALL POTS OF SOUP   97

CHAPTER 4. BOWLS OF COMFORT   113

CHAPTER 5. LOVE FROM THE OVEN 145

CHAPTER 6. BREAD MAKES IT A MEAL 191

CHAPTER 9. A FEW DESSERTS FOR TWO   275

INTRODUCTION

I've come to learn over the years that there is a great amount of fear and avoidance surrounding cooking. I grew up cooking, so I'm a little less fearful than most, but when I think back to those first few years out on my own, in college, I can remember fumbling around in the kitchen. But over the years, as cooking has moved from my hobby to my passion to my full-time job, I've learned that all you need is practice. No one walks into the kitchen a fantastic cook. Nothing about cooking comes naturally—it is like a science experiment that you must perform in the right order or it flops. No one naturally knows how to do science without being taught first, right?

I tackled my trepidation in the kitchen two ways: by watching cooking shows and by practicing. I would watch Rachael Ray or Giada De Laurentiis (often skipping class, ha ha) on TV, and it would fill me with confidence. They made it look so easy! So, I would bounce off the couch and head to the store for ingredients (often, finding unfamiliar ingredients can be the hardest part of cooking!), then come home and try to cook just like them. It wasn't perfect, not even close, but the first time I made a pot of my favorite soup—minestrone, a recipe by Rachael Ray that made 16 servings—I was proud. And then I just kept at it. The more I flexed my cooking muscle, the bigger it became.

To improve, you just gotta get in there and do it. The more you do it, the better you'll get. And then one day you'll wake up and find yourself riffing on your leftovers in the fridge and coming up with a meal on your own. And when that day happens, I want you to step back and celebrate, because cooking is a skill that is hard-won and should be celebrated. So, start with just one day a week. Make dinner. Slow down and enjoy the process.

I've always believed that when learning how to cook, it's best to start small. I started my business sharing small dessert recipes (*Dessert for Two*, actually) and loved that it inspired confidence in the kitchen. It's a lot easier to master a small recipe for four cupcakes rather than try for a large recipe that makes 36 cupcakes and risk a recipe failure. If a small recipe fails, it's a lot fewer wasted ingredients. Once you can confidently make a small recipe, you're ready to scale up.

The recipes in this book can absolutely be scaled up to serve a larger crowd. But if I'm being honest, I created these recipes for small households like mine. I was single and living on my own when I learned how to cook, and, often, cutting a regular recipe in half didn't work. I was inspired to create recipes for households of one or two people. Just because you're not a family of six doesn't mean you don't get to enjoy food!

Most recipes make six to eight servings, which contributes to a lot of food waste, even with a family of four. My recipes aim to make enough food for dinner tonight with the potential of leftovers for lunch the next day. And that's it. No more pans of lasagna that make 17 servings. No more getting tired of leftovers and tossing them in the bin.

I feel so strongly about reducing food waste that I compiled a list of recipes in the back of the book to help you use the remaining portion of food you might have from making one or two recipes. If you have a large bunch of cilantro left over from making my Creamy Chicken Enchiladas, then I want you to know that there are 16 other recipes here to help you use the remaining bundle of herbs, including a cilantro pesto that you'll want to slather on everything.

While I am incredibly blessed that my household of one became a household of three when I got married and had my daughter, we still cook small dinners. We do this mainly because we enjoy cooking together every night. If I make a large recipe for a stew on Monday, we're not only facing leftovers, but we're also limiting our ability to make something new the next night.

Small-batch cooking is in my blood. My grandmother scaled down almost every recipe she made, and I cherish her vintage 6-inch pie pan. I remember her small apple pies that used one or two apples instead of a 5-pound bag.

I come from a semifamous restaurant family in Dallas, and so cooking for people and feeding them well is important to me. I do it with love, and I do it often. My grandma and her sister, Rose, ran a restaurant in Dallas called Rose's Bluebonnet Sandwich Shop. When my mom was little, Rose's was the place where all downtown Dallas workers stopped by for a plate lunch. Rose got up early and flipped the barbecue in the smokers; her arms and hands were black from the smoke. When the original *Bonnie and Clyde* was being filmed in Dallas, she was tasked with feeding the crew during filming. Rose fed people well.

Over the years, Rose's transitioned from barbecue plate lunches to burgers only. After that, my grandma helped Rose fend off the celebrities and press that wanted to sing the praises of the best hamburgers ever because the two of them really couldn't handle any more business. When *D Magazine* would write about her or when Mickey Mantle would tell someone to eat there, the two of them would groan and complain as the line formed out the door. When Don Henley dedicated a song to her burgers at a concert my parents attended, we laughed because we knew Rose was gonna be pissed.

When I was a teenager, I began spending part of my summer in the restaurant during lunch service. I remember my grandma counting tickets at the end of each day, and I recall 75 to 120 burgers was the usual amount.

We called her restaurant Rosie's, never Bluebonnet, and none of us has ever had a better burger anywhere.

Rose passed when I was in college, and, unfortunately, my grandmother passed a few years after that. I didn't quite know that the summers I spent working in her restaurant would mean anything to me later in life. I only knew that all of the adults around me talked frequently about how she should retire and take a break from feeding and serving people. She'd been doing it "too long," in their opinion.

But she didn't. When she called for an ambulance on a Friday afternoon (after lunch service and cleaning up the kitchen), she knew if she went to the hospital, she wouldn't be coming home. She was right.

There are still remnants of Rose in Dallas. I've just moved back to Texas after 12 years away, and I've never felt more comfortable in my own skin in this town. I love Texas with my whole heart. It's an identity for me.

Rose is still a beacon to me and to the city of Dallas. And she did it all with her sister. Neither of them are here anymore to help me with my journey to have a career in the food world, but, as strong women, they would tell me that women don't really need help; we just need time to figure things out.

I've been told that I cook like Rose. I'm a mess in the kitchen. I just throw things together, and somehow, it works. I cook with confidence—I generally know what I'm doing in the kitchen and how it will turn out. I'm not afraid to fail anymore because I'm confident that even my failure will be passable. I'm the person that makes new recipes for company. The stress and anxiety it causes is never worth it, but I do it anyway.

I have things from Rose's and my grandmother's kitchens in my kitchen today. The ladder pictured on page 12 contains the copper salt and pepper shakers that Rose used on her burger patties (complete with the extra large holes my grandpa drilled for her when she complained the shakers weren't quite right). The next basket contains the rolling pins of my great-grandmother Maggie, my Grandmother, and her other sister, Emma. The mustard yellow and pale pink napkins graced the tables of many dinners my grandmother hosted, and I still don't know how she got the fried chicken grease stains out of them because Lord knows I used them for my greasy little fingers as a child.

Continuing on down the ladder you'll find their baking pans and baking utensils (some from my paternal grandmother, too). The last basket is the most special to me. It has a little box of recipes that I hide from sight with that striped kitchen towel. I don't want anyone else's eyes to land on it and decide that it's any less special than I know it to be. The cookbooks next to it are the ones my family used and endlessly adapted to suit their taste.

I hope that my small recipes inspire you to cook more. I hope it's a seed that, once planted, flourishes into a lifelong obsession with food and buckets of confidence to keep doing it your whole life. After all, we have to eat three times a day; shouldn't it be enjoyable?

Love and small casserole dishes,

Christina

A PANTRY FOR TWO

To set yourself up for success in the kitchen, first we need to stock the pantry.

You don't need to stock all of your pantry at once; begin by making a grocery list for ingredients in a few recipes that you want to make, and purchase those ingredients. Check your pantry before your next market trip to ensure you don't buy something you already have on hand.

If you need to use up an ingredient before it spoils, check the Leftovers section at the back of the book (page 311).

Now we're ready to hit the grocery store! The grocery store is my happy place, and I always make the same loop when I'm there. I start in the fresh produce section, spend a few minutes in the dairy and meat section, swoop around to the bulk bins (more on this later), and finally wrap up in the center aisles of the store with the dry goods.

If your grocery store has a bulk bin, you're going to love shopping in it for the majority of your ingredients. This will save you money (zero packaging and advertising expenses lead to lower costs per unit when you buy in bulk). If your store doesn't have a bulk section, be sure to check the unit prices for things like pasta, rice, beans, and grains to see the true price. Local products are always preferred, as are small-batch producers of high-quality, slightly unique or heirloom grains.

Read on for some tips on how to shop for two and avoid food waste, and also for a list of everything I keep in my pantry so that dinners for two come together in a flash.

PRODUCE

Let's talk about produce. It's easy to overbuy produce because it's a good price, and then end up tossing it in the compost bin when you don't use it because you're only cooking for two. It's best to only buy what you need. Resist the temptation to buy more than one cucumber just because they're two for $1 in the summertime. That is, unless you know you have a languishing can of chickpeas in the pantry and that you'll make hummus and use cucumbers as scoops.

When it comes to shopping small for produce, buy organic. Organic produce is usually smaller than its conventional counterpart; plus, as a lady with a background in agriculture, I like to support farmers who choose to grow their crops in this way. That said, I certainly understand that conventional farming practices are necessary, too!

Onions: The ones in the bulk bag are always smaller (and thus, more appropriately sized for two) than the ones sold individually. That said, you can buy one big onion for the week and store the remaining portion of it wrapped tightly in the fridge. A 2-pound bag of onions usually lasts me two weeks if I store them in a cool, dark place. I stock:

- yellow onions (one or two per week)
- red onions (only if it's on the menu plan for the week)
- scallions (one small bunch)

Garlic: The truth is, you just won't use an entire head of garlic in a week or two. If you do, let's be friends, because I really need someone in my life that eats more garlic than I do. The best deal on garlic when you're small-batch cooking is the little jars of prechopped garlic. Ensure they're packed in nothing but oil and store them in the fridge. One teaspoon = one small clove. I stock:

- one small jar of chopped garlic in oil

Sweet potatoes: Every week, I buy a sack of sweet potatoes from Trader Joe's. They're smaller than the sweet potatoes sold individually, and I love to eat one with breakfast (plus butter + cinnamon, of course!). I've even successfully convinced my toddler that a steamed sweet potato is an acceptable snack. (When is my Mom of the Year award coming in the mail?) I plop them on salads and stir them into hot rice. I even make pancakes with them. I go over the best way to roast them in my recipe for Steak and Sweet Potato Bowls with Creamy Kale (page 122). I stock:

- two to four sweet potatoes per week

Bell peppers: I hope your grocery store stocks mini bell peppers. I use them quite a bit because they're perfectly portioned. It also just so happens that my kid eats bell peppers like apples and has since she was 10 months old (weirdo).

If you can't find the mini bell peppers, just use half of the smallest one you can find, and wrap the remaining portion in plastic wrap for storage in the fridge. Save it for another recipe, add it to your scrambled eggs, or use it as a hummus dipper. I stock:

- one bag of mixed mini bell peppers (or 1 red bell pepper)

Carrots: I buy whole organic carrots in a 1-pound bag. The versatility is endless—use them to make stock, peel and slice them for almost any recipe, or whittle them down to smaller sticks for snacks.

Greens: The shelf life of greens in a small household is always on my mind. I buy the smallest amount possible, and I've also found that clamshell containers keep lettuce and greens much fresher than plastic bags where moisture can collect. When I get the greens home from the store, I give them a quick rinse, wrap them in paper towels, and place them in a breathable mesh bag. At the end of the week, if I have any leftover greens, they get added to smoothies or scrambled eggs.

Fresh herbs: I have a fun secret for you: did you know that the potted herbs sold in dirt are actually the cheapest option for you? I keep three little pots in my kitchen filled with soil. I buy the herbs in dirt in the produce section, snip off what I need and plant the rest. No, they don't last forever, but you will get significantly longer shelf life plus less waste. If you've ever thrown away a wilted bag of cilantro and parsley because you couldn't use it within the week, you'll be reaching for mini pots to plant. Plus, they're so pretty in the kitchen!

The types of fresh herbs I keep on hand depends on the season. I stock fresh basil and mint in the summer for salads, pastas, and cocktails. I rely on fresh rosemary, parsley, and oregano in the cooler months to bring flavor to comforting stews and pasta dishes. I use cilantro year-round, but its season is the transitional cool months of the spring and fall. I do grow a lot of my own herbs because I'm lucky enough to live in a mild climate, but most grocery stores stock fresh herbs and herb pastes these days. I stock:

- fresh basil
- fresh rosemary
- fresh parsley
- fresh cilantro
- fresh mint
- fresh oregano

DAIRY AND MEAT

Dairy: I almost always buy the personal-size dairy products. The pint of milk instead of the quart, the personal-size plain yogurt as a healthier sour cream for two, and the smallest block of cheese for shredding. If you look, you will find smaller containers. While it may cost a few more pennies per pound, if you're throwing away a giant tub of unused moldy sour cream at the end of the week, you're not saving money. I stock:

- 6-ounce containers of plain Greek yogurt (I use this for sour cream 90 percent of the time)
- 8-ounce blocks of cheese for grating (I never buy pre-grated cheese with the exception of Parmesan)
- grated Parmesan

- whole milk ricotta (or make your own with my recipe on page 41)
- whole milk

Meat: If you aren't lucky enough to have a meat counter where you can buy a half-pound of meat as called for in my recipes (or, if it's just much more economical to buy in bulk), I promise I will always suggest a way to use up the remaining meat. Check the tips/notes section of a recipe to see how 1 pound of ground turkey goes toward Bourbon-Glazed Turkey Burgers (page 204) and Spaghetti with Small-Batch Meat Sauce (page 32).

I'm also a big fan of using a FoodSaver system to store leftover meats. It creates air-tight and compact packages that are easily stored in the freezer until you need them. I stock:

- ground turkey and beef
- chicken: breasts, thighs (drumsticks occasionally), and a whole chicken for roasting
- fresh sausage in casing, plus kielbasa
- bacon
- thin salami slices
- raw gulf shrimp
- wild salmon

CANNED GOODS AND OTHER DRY GOODS

Tomato products: I can always manage to pull together dinner if I have some sort of canned tomato in my pantry. Even if I just simmer it with a few herbs and spices and pour it over pasta, I've made dinner from scratch rather than going out. I'll give you many more exciting options for a can of tomatoes, but that's still one of my go-tos a few times a month. (Add some ground turkey, and you'll have my favorite small-batch meat sauce page 32). I stock:

- tomato paste
- crushed tomatoes
- tomato sauce
- sun-dried tomatoes packed in oil

I don't use canned diced tomatoes. They contain a chemical (calcium chloride) that helps the chunks of tomatoes hold their shape during cooking, and so they never break down. I want tomatoes that melt into my sauce or stew, and so I reach for crushed tomatoes. If you have trouble finding crushed, whole tomatoes work well, too; just crush them with your hands as you add them to the pot.

The only thing we small households have going for us in the tomato aisle is the small, 8-ounce cans of tomato sauce. I try to use the small can of tomato sauce as often as possible because it's perfectly portioned for us.

As for the other canned tomato products in the aisle, we don't often need the entire can when cooking for two. And furthermore, I've only ever found crushed tomatoes in the giant 28-ounce cans. What to do? I pour the remaining portion of the tomatoes into a glass mason jar, place in the fridge, and make a plan to use it within 5 days (scan the Leftovers section on page 311 for all of my tomato dishes). For tomato paste, scoop it out into 1 tablespoon portions, freeze, and then bag them up. If you can find tomato paste in a tube, grab it!

Chipotles: I know my Texas is showing by how often I use chipotles in my cooking. They're smoky and spicy—a combo of which I can't get enough. I used to buy the canned, whole chipotles packed in adobo sauce because that's all I could find, but now I buy the jar of chopped chipotles in the same adobo sauce. Since they're chopped, I just measure out exactly how much I need and put the rest back in the fridge in my condiment section.

You can find chipotle products in the Latino section of your grocery store. I almost guarantee they have it, but if you cannot find it, chipotle powder can be substituted in a pinch.

Pasta: Probably the thing I make most—a good pasta dinner for two. It's quick, filling, and easy. I don't limit myself to standard wheat pasta. I seek out soba and udon noodles, too. I stock:

- short pastas (like campanelle, penne, ziti)
- long pastas (linguine, spaghetti, fettuccine)
- soba noodles (made from a mix of buckwheat and regular wheat flour)
- udon noodles

Dried herbs: Dried herbs and spices go bad when exposed to air over long periods of time. And a 4-ounce jar of cumin can be hard to get through when cooking for two. For this reason, I buy my spices in bulk. I bring my little glass jars to the grocery store, tare them out on the scale (have an employee do this for you), and then fill them at the store. This way, I don't have any wasted spices or wasted plastic baggies to toss. I stock:

- chili powder
- oregano
- garlic powder
- onion powder
- cayenne pepper
- red pepper flakes
- cumin
- basil
- smoked paprika

Oils: Because oils spoil quickly when exposed to light and air, it's best to only buy small bottles of oil that you use on a regular basis. A high-quality olive oil and neutral oil is all you need (I alternate between avocado, safflower, and canola routinely). The one exception I make is a special container of walnut oil. I find the omega-3s in walnut oil to be worth it, and I store it in the fridge until the next time I make French Lentils and Kielbasa (page 80). I stock:

- extra virgin olive oil
- safflower oil (or avocado, sunflower, or canola)
- walnut oil

Vinegars: My favorite way to add punch to a recipe without using salt is vinegar. I stock:

- brown rice vinegar
- balsamic vinegar
- red wine vinegar
- apple cider vinegar

Beans and legumes: I am the biggest fan of beans you'll ever meet. I love beans so much that I refuse to buy them from the can. I soak and make my own from scratch. This process has become much easier lately because I invested in a pressure cooker! (I personally use the mini 3-quart Instant Pot.) I soak 1 cup of beans overnight and pressure-cook them in 15 minutes. If I forget to soak them, then I pressure cook for an extra 10 minutes. Easy! However, you may absolutely buy canned beans whenever called for in these recipes. Canned beans are significantly easier and quicker to deal with, but I prefer the texture and flavor of fresh. I stock:

- black beans
- chickpeas
- cannellini (white) beans
- kidney beans (for Minestrone/Ribollita, page 106)
- green lentils

Grains: Another endorsement for the bulk bin section at your store, grains are great to buy in bulk. I use an assortment of grains in my cooking to keep things exciting and new. They're a great alternative to meat, and I never seem to get bored with grains the way I do with chicken.

I stock:

- quinoa
- polenta (coarsely ground cornmeal)
- basmati rice
- arborio rice (or canaroli for making risotto)
- barley

Bread: Bread is so difficult to use up in a timely manner in a small household. Often, the package or loaf goes stale before it can be consumed. It's the main reason I included a chapter on small-batch bread recipes at the end of this book. When I'm not baking small-batch bread recipes, I buy:

- corn and flour tortillas (refrigerated, these last a while, but they must be warmed up before use)
- half loaves of sliced bread from the deli section of the grocery store
- small baguettes (remaining portion wrapped twice in plastic and stored in the freezer)
- packages of four sub rolls (freeze the remaining two for another night)

A FEW PIECES OF EQUIPMENT

When cooking for two, you'll need some smaller pans and a few smaller pots. These are my favorite picks.

Mini Dutch oven: When I found out that Dutch ovens came in a smaller 3.5-quart size, I had to resist the urge to buy them in almost every color available. I love the enamel-coated cast-iron Dutch ovens made by Le Creuset because they're oven safe and perfect for small-batch soups, stews, and no-knead bread.

8-inch square pan: While most casserole recipes are baked in a 9-by-13-inch pan, we'll be using an 8-inch square pan to bake our smaller versions.

8-inch skillet: Since I've devoted a large section of the book to "one-pan meals," a high-quality 8-inch skillet is imperative. Try to get one that's non-stick and one that isn't, and make sure the handles are oven-safe, as quite a few recipes are finished in the oven.

Cast-iron skillet: Some food just tastes better in a cast-iron skillet, but that's entirely a preference decided by my Southern tongue. If you already have one nonstick skillet and are looking for a second regular skillet, try a small cast-iron skillet.

Food processor: I use a food processor quite a bit, and a small one that holds about 4 cups is perfect for my recipes.

Small baking dishes (ramekins, small casseroles): When seeking small baking dishes, check for ramekins with 10-ounce capacities, small decorative bakeware, and any other oven-safe dish with a 1- to 2-quart capacity.

Instant Pot Mini (electric pressure cooker): While the Instant Pot wasn't the first electric pressure cooker on the market, I firmly believe it's the safest and easiest to use. I'm so grateful they decided to make a small one with a 3-quart capacity. I use it frequently for making stock and beans to use in other

recipes. I really love its efficiency at making caramelized onions in a fraction of the time!

Saucepan: The pan that you commonly cook rice in, about 2 quarts, is the perfect saucepan that we will use for small dinners.

Standard roasting pans with a rim: Bad roasting pans are one of my pet peeves. When I was a private chef, I traveled with my roasting pans because they were thick and had a 1-inch rim all the way around the sides. Seek thick metal pans (no insulated pans here) and ones with a rim so roasted vegetables don't slide off the edges.

Fondue pot: Entirely optional, but so fun! I've included our favorite recipe for Classic Cheese Fondue for Two on page 172. It's a fun, romantic dinner to celebrate your anniversary or Valentine's Day. I prefer fondue pots that are stove-top safe, meaning you can use the vessel on the stove for making the actual fondue. Then, once it's done, it moves back to the unit with a small heat source underneath. Mine is made by Le Creuset and is very heavy and durable.

Thermometer: If you're up for my small-batch bread recipes in the last chapter of this book, you'll need a cooking thermometer to ensure the liquids are the right temperature for yeast to thrive.

CHAPTER 1.
PASTA FOR TWO

We are starting with two-person pasta dinners because pasta is our go-to meal plan several nights each week. Two bowls of delicious pasta is how we frequently begin and end our workweek. Monday-night pasta is my favorite comforting dinner, and pasta on Friday nights is so easy that I hardly have to think about it at the end of a long week. Plus, we never grow tired of new ways to enjoy pasta. These recipes call for a few different types of pasta to yield exciting, creamy bowls that you will love. Many of the pasta bowls are vegetarian, so add sliced chicken, crumbled sausage, or a fried egg to suit your taste.

Spaghetti with Small-Batch Meat Sauce

There's something so comforting to me about a plate of spaghetti with meat sauce. I even prefer it to chicken soup when I'm sick. The problem is, most meat sauce recipes make several quarts of sauce and take hours to make.

This meat sauce comes together in about 45 minutes and makes enough for two meals. I serve it with spaghetti the first night; on the second night, I either serve it with ricotta gnocchi (page 48) or use it as sauce on a Pizza Baguettes (page 207). The extra freezes very well, too! I make it in my 2-quart saucepan, and I use the lid to help with splattering while cooking.

1 tablespoon olive oil

½ pound ground beef or ground turkey

½ small onion, diced

One 6-ounce can tomato paste

½ teaspoon salt

½ teaspoon freshly ground black pepper

1 garlic clove, minced

1 teaspoon dried basil

1 teaspoon dried oregano

One 15-ounce can crushed tomatoes

1 small red bell pepper, diced

⅓ cup grated Pecorino Romano, plus extra for serving

½ cup dry red wine

Cooked spaghetti, for serving

In a 2-quart saucepan (yes, this is a much smaller pan than you would normally use for making meat sauce), add the olive oil.

Turn the heat to medium-high and add the ground beef. Use a wooden spoon to break up the beef into smaller pieces while it cooks.

Once the beef is browned, add the onion and tomato paste. Cook for about 3 to 4 minutes, until the tomato paste starts to darken slightly.

Add all the remaining ingredients.

Give it a good stir and bring the mixture to a simmer. Place a lid on the pan, lower the heat to medium-low, and let it cook for 30 minutes.

Remove the lid and stir the sauce a few times to make sure it isn't sticking to the bottom.

Serve with cooked spaghetti, topped with extra Romano.

Spinach Pesto Pasta with Walnuts

My mother-in-law taught me her method for cooking pasta in a small pot with chicken broth. The end result is pasta coated with a silky sauce because, as the pasta cooks and absorbs the chicken broth, it releases starch that forms a sauce. While I could eat the pasta as-is right out of the pot in its silky, salty glory, I stir in my spinach pesto.

Pesto is my favorite method for getting a leafy green into my loved ones. Instead of using all basil for my pesto, I use baby spinach with a handful of basil leaves. The sun-dried tomatoes give the sauce body and help it cling to the cooked pasta. The final touch of feta and walnuts lends so much crunch.

2 cups chicken broth

8 ounces penne pasta

2½ ounces baby spinach (about half a 5-ounce bag)

¼ cup sun-dried tomatoes, plus extra for serving

1 garlic clove

½ cup grated Parmesan

½ cup walnuts, toasted, plus extra for serving

⅓ cup plus 1 tablespoon olive oil

15 large basil leaves

½ teaspoon salt

Freshly ground black pepper

¼ cup crumbled feta cheese

In a small saucepan with a tight-fitting lid, combine the chicken broth and pasta.

Turn the heat to medium and cook, stirring occasionally, until the mixture comes to a simmer.

Once simmering, stir and then cover with the lid. Allow the pasta to cook with the lid on, but check on it every few minutes and stir to make sure it won't stick to the bottom of the pan.

Once most of the broth is absorbed, taste the pasta. It should be al dente. If not, add another splash of broth, cover, and cook until it is.

Meanwhile, combine the spinach, sun-dried tomatoes, garlic, Parmesan, walnuts, oil, basil, salt, and a few grinds of black pepper in the bowl of a food processor. Pulse until the pesto is smooth.

When the pasta is al dente, stir in about half of the pesto (save the rest for another use; see Tips for Leftovers below) and toss to combine.

Plate the pasta and top with crumbled feta and extra walnuts or sun-dried tomatoes.

Pear and Parmesan Pasta Salad

Now that you have the rest of the bag of baby spinach to use after making spinach pesto, I'm begging you to make my favorite weekday lunch/picnic pasta salad/take-along side dish recipe: this pasta salad with pear, Parmesan, walnuts, and spinach.

To make the Parmesan chunks that are so delicious in this salad, take a large piece of Parmesan and use the tip of a small knife to break off bite-size chunks. When Parmesan is "cut" this way, you can enjoy the salt crystals that form in the cheese.

6 ounces farfalle pasta

¼ cup walnut pieces

2½ ounces baby spinach (about half a 5-ounce bag)

½ cup Parmesan chunks

1 large ripe pear (I like an extra ripe Bartlett pear), core removed and thinly sliced

Salt

Freshly ground black pepper

In a large pot, bring plenty of water to a boil.

Salt the water and cook the pasta according to the package directions.

Reserve ½ cup of the pasta water and then drain the pasta.

Meanwhile, add the walnut pieces to a dry skillet and toast over medium heat until fragrant and starting to brown around the edges. Immediately remove the nuts from the skillet to a small bowl to cool.

Toss the drained pasta with all the remaining ingredients, adding enough pasta water to coat everything.

Taste and add any additional salt and pepper.

This salad is great served room temperature or cold.

Baked Ziti with Homemade Ricotta

Much like lasagna, most recipes for baked ziti make an entire 9-by-13-inch tray that serves at least eight people. And while it is delicious, the small household will be tired of leftovers by day three. And that's a fact.

I scaled down this baked ziti to a 9-by-5-inch loaf pan, but you can also use two oversized 10-ounce ramekins instead.

Use your favorite jar of marinara sauce here, but also don't miss the add-ins that make this extra special: an extra dose of oregano, garlic powder, and fresh basil leaves stuffed between the pasta.

Butter

1 tablespoon olive oil

¼ pound bulk sausage (or 1 link)

1 cup jarred marinara sauce

⅛ teaspoon dried oregano

⅛ teaspoon granulated garlic powder

6 ounces ziti pasta

¼ cup Homemade Ricotta (recipe follows) or 2 ounces store-bought whole milk ricotta (see Note on page 42), plus extra for layering

4 ounces fresh mozzarella, diced

4 to 6 fresh basil leaves

Preheat the oven to 350°F and generously butter two 10-ounce ramekins or a 9-by-5-inch loaf pan.

In a small skillet over medium heat, add the olive oil and heat through for a few seconds. Add the sausage to the pan if you're using bulk sausage or squeeze to remove the sausage from its casing. Break up the sausage with a wooden spoon while it cooks.

Once the sausage is browned, add the marinara, oregano, and garlic to the pan. Stir to combine, and then turn off the heat.

Meanwhile, bring a salted pot of water to a rolling boil and cook the pasta 2 minutes shy of the recommended cooking time. Drain the pasta.

In a bowl, stir together the pasta and the marinara mixture. Add the ricotta and stir to combine. Add the fresh mozzarella cubes to the bowl, but save a few for the top of the pan.

Layer half of the pasta mixture into the baking pan. Spoon extra ricotta dollops over the pasta. Tear the fresh basil leaves and poke them between the pasta. Top with the remaining pasta.

Top the pan (or each ramekin) with the remaining mozzarella. Bake the pan or ramekins for 20 to 25 minutes, until the cheese on top is golden brown.

Homemade Ricotta

If I knew that homemade ricotta was made with just two ingredients, milk and lemon juice, I would have started making it for myself years ago!

This is a smal-batch recipe that is perfect for stirring into the Pasta Primavera with Homemade Ricotta (recipe follows), but it's easily doubled or tripled to yield more cheese.

Homemade ricotta can be as thick or as creamy as you like. For a texture most similar to store-bought ricotta, only let it drain for 10 minutes. For a thicker texture, up to an hour.

Stir in the salt just before serving. Oh, and save the liquid (also called whey) that drains off the cheese to use in smoothies or for your next batch of Perfect Dinner Rolls (on page 264). Whey is full of protein and calcium, which makes for very tender bread dough.

2 cups whole milk (not ultra-pasteurized, check the label)
1 tablespoon fresh lemon juice
¼ teaspoon sea salt

Set up a strainer lined with a few layers of cheesecloth over a bowl. Set it aside.

In a saucepan, heat the milk to 200°F. Stir it occasionally and keep an eye on it so it doesn't boil over.

When the milk reaches 200°F, turn off the heat and stir in the lemon juice.

Let the pan sit undisturbed for 10 minutes.

Pour the mixture through the cheesecloth-lined strainer.

Let it drain for 10 minutes for a creamy texture, or longer for a firmer texture.

Stir in the salt just before serving.

Pasta Primavera with Homemade Ricotta

Put your fresh homemade ricotta to use in this lovely and light pasta dish. This easy dish shines with fresh spring vegetables from the farmers' market. Pencil-thin asparagus spears, fresh peas, and baby carrots are so sweet and totally worth the early morning trek to the market. 6 ounces spaghetti

½ cup thinly sliced carrots
½ cup frozen peas
8 spears of fresh asparagus
10 sugar snap peas
1 cup Homemade Ricotta
    (recipe page 41) or 8 ounces
    store-bought whole milk
    ricotta (see Note)
¼ cup grated Parmesan
Freshly ground black pepper

Bring a large pot of salted water to a boil over high heat.

Once the water is boiling, cook the pasta according to the package directions. About 2 minutes before the pasta is done, add the carrots, peas, asparagus, and sugar snap peas to the water. Continue to cook until the pasta is done and the veggies are crisp-to-tender. Most likely, the water will come back up to a boil and it will need 1 minute of boiling to cook everything through.

Drain the pasta and vegetables and place it in a serving bowl. Add the ricotta and toss to coat the pasta with the mixture. Stir in the Parmesan and taste to adjust for salt and pepper.

NOTE: You can absolutely use store-bought whole milk ricotta for this recipe. It will probably need a touch more salt than the homemade version.

Caramelized Onion and Swiss Chard Fettuccine

I make this cozy, creamy, and slightly sweet pasta dinner when the Swiss chard leaves in the garden are as big as an open sunflower. I love it so much, and it is my belief that kids can enjoy it (provided they don't mind "green flecks") because of the sweetness of the caramelized onions.

That said, if you don't have a garden, most bunches of Swiss chard contain four to six leaves, and this recipe only uses two. To utilize the rest of the bunch, I chop up the leaves (stems discarded) and freeze them. Use them any place you would use frozen spinach. As for the stems, I don't really discard them . . . they're great hidden in a pressed juice or smoothie. They hardly have a flavor but have tons of beta-carotene!

Taste the pasta once you stir it all together—if it tastes too sweet, add a bit more salt and Parmesan. The flavors of sweet, salty, and earthy should be balanced.

6 ounces fettuccine
2 large Swiss chard leaves
½ cup caramelized onions
   (recipe follows)
¼ cup grated Parmesan, plus
   more to taste
3 tablespoons heavy cream
Freshly ground black pepper
Salt

Bring a large pot of salted water to a boil and cook the pasta according to the package directions.

Meanwhile, remove the stems and ribs from the Swiss chard and chop the remaining leafy portions into bite-size pieces. Have the remaining ingredients ready.

When the pasta is done cooking, turn off the heat. Reserve ½ cup of the pasta water and then drain the pasta.

Place the pasta back into the pot and add the reserved pasta water, chard, caramelized onions, Parmesan, cream, black pepper, and a big pinch of salt. Stir quickly, and then place the lid on it.

Let the pasta sit (you're wilting the chard leaves now) for about 3 minutes. Uncover and stir to combine. Add salt and additional Parmesan to taste (see tasting notes above).

Pressure Cooker Caramelized Onions

I was an early adopter of the modern pressure cooker, called the Instant Pot. I saw its potential for making quick work of vegetable scraps for stock and cooking beans in a fraction of the time.

The minute I used it to make a big batch of caramelized onions was when I realized its full potential. I use the Instant Pot Mini with a 3-quart capacity because I'm only cooking for two, but this method works with any pressure cooker.

I make a big batch of Instant Pot caramelized onions, often using the entire 2-pound bag of onions from the market, and store them in ½-cup portions in the freezer for future meals.

While they're delicious stirred into the Caramelized Onion and Swiss Chard Fettuccine on page 44, don't miss their shining moment in Bourbon-Glazed Turkey Burgers (page 204) and on a classy Turkey Apple Butter Grilled Cheese (page 203).

1 tablespoon unsalted butter

2 pounds yellow onions, thinly sliced into half-moon shapes

¼ teaspoon baking soda

Electric Pressure Cooker (Instant Pot):

Turn the electric pressure cooker (Instant Pot) to "Sauté." Add the butter and let it melt before stirring in the sliced onions.

Cook the onions until they're slightly softened and starting to release their juices. Then stir in the baking soda and 2 tablespoons of water.

Place the lid on the pressure cooker and turn the pressure valve to "Seal." Press "Pressure Cook" and enter 15 minutes.

When the timer goes off, do a natural pressure release until the pressure valve drops. Remove the lid of the pressure cooker and stir the onions.

Press "Sauté" again, and cook the onions while stirring frequently until they caramelize and turn a light golden brown. It will take about 10 to 15 minutes.

Let the onions cool completely, and then package them in ½-cup portions to store in the freezer for future use.

Stovetop:

To make caramelized onions without an electric pressure cooker (Instant Pot), melt the butter in a large cast-iron skillet over medium heat. Add the onions, and cook until slightly softened and starting to release their juices. Then stir in the baking soda and 2 tablespoons of water. Lower the heat to medium-low and continue to cook while stirring occasionally for about 35 to 45 minutes. The onions are done when they're golden brown.

Gnocchi, Three Ways

I have always loved gnocchi, but the classic version made with potatoes is a bit too finicky for me. Instead, I use ricotta. They're just as light and fluffy but a bit creamier!

Let's start with the classic ricotta gnocchi. I make these frequently because they come together quickly. They're great with a basic meat sauce (as on page 32), in soup as dumplings, or with an easy brown butter sauce.

4 ounces whole milk ricotta (store-bought or homemade on page 41)

1 large egg

¼ cup grated Parmesan

½ teaspoon salt

¼ teaspoon freshly ground black pepper

1 garlic clove, grated on a microplane

1 cup all-purpose flour, plus more for dusting and rolling

In a medium bowl, stir together the ricotta, egg, Parmesan, salt, pepper, and grated garlic. Mix very well.

Next, gently stir in the flour, just until streaks of flour disappear, being careful not to overmix or the gnocchi will be tough.

Once the dough comes together, lightly flour a work surface and scoop out one-quarter of the mixture. Dust flour on the top, and with flour-dusted hands, gently roll the dough into a 1-inch log that is about 8 inches long—the length will depend on exactly how much dough you grab; just make sure the diameter of the rope is 1 inch. Keep the remaining dough covered with a damp kitchen towel while you work.

Cut the log into 1-inch pieces (or any size you like your gnocchi), and set aside on a flour-dusted plate.

Repeat with the remaining dough until all of the gnocchi are made. You should get about 50 gnocchi.

There are two ways to cook gnocchi:

Bring a large pot of salted water to a boil and add the gnocchi when the water begins to boil. Let them cook for about 60 seconds; when they float, they're done. Drain and serve with desired sauce. The Small-Batch Meat Sauce on page 32 is perfect!

Or, melt half a stick of butter in a nonstick skillet and cook the gnocchi on each side in batches until they are golden brown. Top with a handful (around 1/3 cup) of crumbled cheese (blue cheese is good) and something crunchy (like a small handful of toasted walnuts).

Beet Gnocchi

My toddler loves the color pink, so it's actually been easy to get her to enjoy beets. These beet gnocchi are one of her favorite dinners, and I love to serve them for a romantic dinner, too. The fuchsia color is just begging to be served on Valentine's Day.

One important note: I don't recommend using precooked beets for this dish, because they have a tendency to be an unattractive shade of brown. A fresh beet will yield the brightest pink gnocchi.

1 small beet, peeled and chopped into 1-inch pieces

4 ounces whole milk ricotta (store-bought or homemade on page 41)

1 garlic clove, grated on a microplane

¾ teaspoon salt

½ teaspoon freshly ground black pepper

1 large egg

1 cup all-purpose flour, plus more for dusting and rolling

ZA'ATAR BUTTER SAUCE

4 tablespoons butter

1 tablespoon olive oil

4 tablespoons za'atar

First, steam the beet pieces until soft, either by using a vegetable steamer basket or by wrapping in foil and baking in the oven at 375°F for about 40 minutes.

Next add the steamed beet pieces, ricotta, garlic, salt, pepper, and egg to the bowl of a food processor. Pulse until everything is very well incorporated.

Pour the mixture into a bowl and add the flour. Gently stir the flour in, being careful not to overmix.

Proceed with the directions for the ricotta gnocchi above.

These beet gnocchi are delicious served in a warm butter za'atar sauce. To make the sauce, melt the butter and oil in a 10-inch skillet until it starts to sizzle. Add the za'atar and fry until fragrant, about 20 seconds. Add the beet gnocchi to the pan and cook on each side in batches until they are golden brown.

NOTE: These beet gnocchi are delicious boiled briefly until they float, then fried lightly in a skillet with half a stick of butter and a generous tablespoon of za'atar.

Pumpkin Gnocchi

These pumpkin gnocchi are on heavy rotation in our house during the fall months. I always seem to have a can of pumpkin open for pumpkin pancakes and pumpkin quick bread. Make sure you're using canned plain pumpkin, not pumpkin pie filling.

4 ounces whole milk ricotta (store-bought or homemade on page 41)

⅓ cup canned pumpkin

1 garlic clove, grated on a microplane

¾ teaspoon salt

½ teaspoon freshly ground black pepper

1 large egg

1 cup all-purpose flour, plus more for dusting and rolling

SAGE BUTTER SAUCE

4 tablespoons salted butter

1 tablespoon olive oil

8 fresh sage leaves, for serving

Parmesan shavings, for serving

Follow the directions for the ricotta gnocchi above, but include the pumpkin in the mixing stage.

These pumpkin gnocchi are delicious served in a warm sage butter sauce. To make it, melt the butter and oil in a 10-inch skillet until it starts to sizzle. Add the fresh sage leaves and fry until crispy, about 20 seconds.

Remove the sage leaves and set them aside for garnish.

Cook the gnocchi on each side in batches until they are golden brown.

Serve with the sage leaves, butter from the pan drizzled on top, and Parmesan shavings.

Lemon Spaghetti with Artichokes and Bread Crumbs

My love for artichokes knows no limits, but if you don't feel the same way, proceed with this recipe without them. You'll end up with a lemony spaghetti with bread crumbs on top. If you're looking for a way to dress this recipe up a bit, a scoop of mascarpone stirred in is incredible.

FOR THE BREAD CRUMBS

2 tablespoons olive oil

⅓ cup bread crumbs

Salt

Freshly ground black pepper

FOR THE REST

1 tablespoon olive oil

2 garlic cloves, minced

¼ teaspoon red pepper flakes, plus more to taste

¾ cup dry white wine

8 ounces artichoke hearts (defrosted, if frozen)

Salt

Freshly ground black pepper

8 ounces spaghetti

Zest of 1 lemon

½ cup Parmesan

⅓ cup mascarpone (optional)

First, make the toasted bread crumbs: In a large skillet, heat the olive oil over medium heat. Add the bread crumbs and toast, stirring frequently, until they're golden brown. Add a pinch of salt and pepper and remove from the heat. Remove from the pan to cool and set aside.

Meanwhile, bring a large pot of salted water to a boil. Cook the spaghetti according to the package directions. Drain and set aside.

In the same pan used for the bread crumbs, make the rest of the pasta sauce: Add the olive oil and turn the heat to medium. Sauté the garlic and red pepper flakes.

Add the artichoke hearts to the pan in a single layer and sear on one side until golden brown.

Next, add the wine and a pinch of salt and pepper to the pan. Cook until the artichokes are tender.

Add the drained pasta to the skillet with the artichokes and toss to combine. Stir in the lemon zest and Parmesan (and optional mascarpone). Taste and adjust for additional salt, pepper, and red pepper flakes, if desired.

Linguine with Roasted Red Onions, Fresh Oregano, and Lemon Zest

If you're anything like me, the onion bits on a tray of roasted veggies are the best bits. And if we take it even further, roasted red onions are the best onions to roast. The high sugar content in a red onion intensifies even more in the oven.

I toss roasted red onions with freshly cooked hot linguine to create the pasta bowl of my dreams. Fresh oregano, lemon zest, and feta play very important roles here, as does the pasta water at the end.

1 large red onion, washed and cut into wedges (skin left on)
1 tablespoon olive oil
Salt
Freshly ground black pepper
8 sprigs fresh thyme
6 ounces linguine
Zest of 1 lemon
½ cup crumbled feta cheese
3 sprigs fresh oregano

Preheat the oven to 425°F and line a roasting pan with parchment paper.

Place the onion wedges on the baking sheet and toss with the olive oil, a big pinch of salt, freshly ground black pepper, and the thyme sprigs.

Roast the onions for about 22 to 25 minutes, until golden brown in several spots. Let them cool slightly before slicing the ends off and peeling away the papery parts. Separate the onions into bite-size pieces and set aside.

Meanwhile, bring a large pot of salted water to a boil. Cook the pasta according to the package directions.

Once the pasta is done, reserve about ¾ cup of the pasta water.

Drain and pour the hot pasta into a serving bowl. Add the onions, lemon zest, feta, and about ½ cup of the pasta water and toss to combine everything. Add additional water if it seems dry and add the oregano leaves. Toss until the feta starts to melt and the pasta comes together. Taste and add salt and freshly ground black pepper to your liking.

Baked Spaghetti

After I had my daughter, any dish that included baked pasta was so comforting to me. I don't know if it was all the carbs, the cheese, or just the warmth of the dish, but I found a new appreciation for baked pasta.

My favorite was a baked spaghetti dish made in a deep-dish pie plate crammed with so many cheeses that I don't know how my sweet neighbor got it through my doorway. It was excellent.

Here, I've scaled it down to a small skillet and tried to minimize the number of dishes required to make the meal. Since we're browning the meat and tossing the cooked pasta with the sauce in the skillet, we might as well bake the final dish in the skillet, too, right? Make sure your skillet has an oven-safe handle. Also, make sure the cream cheese and ricotta are at room temperature before tossing.

6 ounces spaghetti

1 tablespoon olive oil

½ pound ground turkey or beef

¼ teaspoon salt

Freshly ground black pepper

2 cups jarred marinara sauce

2 ounces cream cheese, at room temperature

½ cup ricotta, at room temperature (store-bought or homemade on page 41)

½ cup shredded mozzarella

Bring a large pot of salted water to a boil. Cook the spaghetti according to the package directions. Drain and set aside.

Preheat the oven to 350°F.

Meanwhile, in an oven-safe skillet, heat the olive oil over medium-high heat. Add the ground turkey (or beef) and cook while breaking it up with a wooden spoon until it's no longer pink.

Add the salt, pepper, and marinara sauce to the pan, and heat to warm through. Remove the pan from the heat, add the cream cheese and ricotta, and stir to melt.

Add the spaghetti to the pan with the sauce and toss to combine. Evenly sprinkle the mozzarella on top, then slide the pan into the oven.

Bake for 15 minutes, or until the cheese melts and the pasta is heated through.

Serve immediately. Leftovers firm up when chilled, so reheat them on the stove.

CHAPTER 2.
SKILLET MEALS

These easy skillet meals are familiar dishes that usually require several pans or bowls to make, such as Chicken Parmesan Meatballs, Sloppy Joe Tater Tot Skillet, and Egg Roll Bowls, but are now made in just one skillet. It's not that I'm lazy, it's just that after a delicious dinner and a glass of wine, nothing is more unappealing than a pile of dirty dishes in my sink! There are also one-pan versions of our favorite things to order at restaurants, including a creamy chicken skillet, a cheater's version of bulgogi, and a steak dinner that technically requires two pans but doesn't require a restaurant reservation. While these recipes are a breeze to make and light on the clean-up, they're still romantic enough for date night at home.

One-Pot Crispy Salami and Cherry Tomato Pasta

I first saw this incredible recipe for pasta and sauce cooked in the same pot in *Martha Stewart Living* magazine. It's equal parts genius (because, hello, one less pan to wash) and unbelievable (raw, uncooked pasta cooks right in the same pan as the sauce!). Since trying Martha's simple version, I've come up with my own.

I like to divide the chop and prep for this recipe between my husband and me to make for a date night in the kitchen. I gather the ingredients and assemble the pan while my husband slices the onions and garlic and gathers the basil from the garden. Whoever finishes their job first gets to pour the rest of the wine into two glasses.

4 ounces thinly sliced dry
   salami

8 ounces cherry tomatoes

1 small onion, sliced

2 garlic cloves, thinly sliced

6 ounces linguine

½ teaspoon red pepper flakes

1 teaspoon salt

¼ teaspoon freshly ground
   black pepper

1 tablespoon olive oil

3 sprigs fresh basil, plus extra
   for serving

¼ cup white wine

First, slice the salami into 1-inch strips. Add them to a straight-sided 3-quart skillet and turn the heat to medium. Let them cook and crisp for a few minutes on each side. (Yes, there's really no need for oil in the pan.)

Stir the salami strips occasionally for about 4 minutes, and when they're starting to turn lightly golden brown, remove them from the skillet with a slotted spoon and place them on a paper towel–lined plate to drain.

Add all of the remaining ingredients to the same skillet (no need to clean it) with 2 cups of water. Break up the linguine to make it fit in the pan.

Turn the heat to medium-high, and cook the mixture while stirring frequently for about 9 minutes. The pasta will soften and soak up the liquid, and the vegetables will cook down.

Test the pasta before turning off the heat—it should be al dente, and all of the liquid should be absorbed. Add the salami back to the pan and stir to integrate.

Divide the mixture between two serving plates and top with more fresh basil.

Cheesy Broccoli Quinoa

When we talk about eating our veggies, things like carrots, peas, and broccoli come to mind. But really, I think an undervalued part of the vegetable equation is alliums—things like onions and garlic. The organosulfur compounds in alliums are amazing for our immune systems—I tend to make this dinner a lot in the wintertime with frozen broccoli.

Any leftovers are amazing mixed with an egg, shaped into patties, and sautéed in a skillet with olive oil. In fact, you might as well double it and plan on that. This dish is great with some grilled chicken stirred in, too!

You need a 2-quart saucepan with a tight-fitting lid for this recipe—the same pot you make rice in.

½ medium onion, diced

1 tablespoon olive oil

2 garlic cloves, minced

½ teaspoon salt

¼ teaspoon freshly ground black pepper

¼ teaspoon dried thyme

½ teaspoon mustard powder

1 cup vegetable broth

½ cup dry white quinoa

1½ cups chopped broccoli florets

¾ cup grated Cheddar

1 scallion, thinly sliced

¼ cup Greek yogurt

Preheat a 2-quart saucepan over medium heat.

Add the olive oil and the diced onions. Sauté for at least 5 minutes, stirring often to prevent the onions from browning on the edges. You really want to soften the onions, so lower the heat if they threaten to burn.

Stir in the garlic, salt, pepper, thyme, and mustard powder. Cook for about 1 minute before stirring in the broth and quinoa.

Bring the mixture to a gentle simmer, lower the heat, cover, and cook for 10 minutes.

Quickly lift the lid and toss the broccoli on top of the quinoa, then close the lid to continue cooking for another 5 minutes.

Remove the lid again and stir. All of the liquid should be absorbed, and the quinoa should be cooked through—if not, cover and cook another 1 to 3 minutes.

Remove the pan from the heat and stir in the Cheddar, scallion, and yogurt.

Mexican Quinoa with Avocado

If you would like a glimpse into my everyday life, look no further than this quinoa bowl. This is what I make for dinner at least one night a week. It's effortless, and I always seem to have the ingredients on hand.

This dish is endlessly versatile: substitute cayenne pepper for jalapeños, leave out the bell pepper if you're lacking, whatever you need to do to make this recipe happen.

Oh, and if you are using a bell pepper, slice up the other half to put out with hummus as a snack while you cook.

1 tablespoon olive oil

2 garlic cloves, minced

½ orange bell pepper, chopped

1 jalapeño, minced (or pinch of cayenne pepper)

1 teaspoon chili powder

1 teaspoon ground cumin

1 teaspoon dried oregano

½ cup white quinoa, rinsed

½ cup vegetable broth (or water)

¾ cup canned crushed tomatoes

¾ cup black beans

½ cup frozen corn kernels

½ teaspoon salt

¼ teaspoon freshly ground black pepper

Small handful cilantro, chopped

Avocado, for serving

Sour cream, for serving

In a 2-quart saucepan, heat the olive oil over medium heat.

Add the garlic, bell pepper, and jalapeño (if using), and sauté for 1 minute.

Add the spices and sauté for another minute.

Next, add the quinoa, broth, tomatoes, beans, corn, salt, and pepper. Give it a good stir, lower the heat to a bare simmer, and place the lid on the pan to cook for 15 minutes.

Check after 15 minutes; the liquid should be completely absorbed and the quinoa should be done.

Remove from the heat and stir in the chopped cilantro. Serve with avocado chunks and sour cream.

Chicken Lettuce Cups

This is one of our favorite appetizers to order at a restaurant during the hot summer months, and so we turned it into a meal we can enjoy at home together on a date night in.

Many chicken lettuce cups recipes feature water chestnuts, but I've replaced them with quick-pickled carrots (from the Almost Korean Beef Bowls on page 116), and I think you'll love it!

Handful of pickled carrots
  (page 116)
3 tablespoons hoisin sauce
1 tablespoon soy sauce
1 tablespoon rice wine vinegar
1 teaspoon sesame oil
1 teaspoon corn starch
3 teaspoons neutral oil, divided
½ pound ground chicken
4 ounces fresh mushrooms,
  cleaned and chopped
1 small carrot, grated
2 garlic cloves, chopped
2 teaspoons freshly grated
  ginger
2 scallions, white and green
  parts sliced and separated
Freshly ground black pepper
Salt
1 small head Bibb lettuce, for
  serving

Chop the pickled carrots into bite-size pieces or smaller, depending on your preference. Set them aside.

In a small bowl, whisk together the hoisin, soy, rice wine vinegar, sesame oil, and corn starch. Set aside.

In a large skillet over medium-high heat, add 2 teaspoons of the neutral oil and heat it for a few seconds. Add the chicken and cook, breaking it up with a wooden spoon, until completely cooked through.

Remove the chicken from the pan and set aside.

Place the pan back on the heat and add the remaining teaspoon of oil. Add the mushrooms, grated carrot, garlic, ginger, and white parts of the scallions. Cook until the mushrooms soften and shrink in size, about 5 minutes. Stir occasionally.

Add the chicken and hoisin sauce mixture to the pan and cook for 2 minutes, Add salt and pepper to the pan and adjust to your taste.

Pour the chicken mixture into a serving bowl. Sprinkle the pickled carrots and the green part of the scallions on top.

Separate the Bibb lettuce into pieces and place four pieces on each plate.

Spoon the chicken into the lettuce cups and serve.

Mexican Street Corn Tacos

If you've never had Mexican street corn (*elotes*), then be prepared to have the best corn of your life. It's charred on the grill and smothered in a creamy cheese sauce with chili powder and lime. It's positively addicting, and the only way to enjoy it more is to wrap it in a tortilla and call it a taco.

4 ears fresh corn, shucked and silks removed

1 tablespoon neutral oil

1 tablespoon sour cream

2 tablespoons mayonnaise

Juice of ½ lime

1 garlic clove, minced

½ teaspoon chili powder

¼ cup crumbled cotija (or feta cheese)

Salt

4 to 6 corn tortillas

1 scallion, sliced, for serving

Cilantro leaves, for serving

You can either grill this corn on a charcoal grill or in a grill pan indoors, your choice.

Either way, heat the grill or pan to high.

Brush the corn with the oil and place it on the grates/in the pan.

Cook each side of the corn until it's blackened in several places; it will pop and spatter as it cooks—be careful!

When each side has several charred places, remove the corn from the heat and let it cool.

In a medium bowl, whisk together the sour cream, mayo, lime juice, garlic, and chili powder.

Slice the corn off the cob and add the kernels to the sour cream sauce. Add the cotija, stir to combine, and then taste the mixture. The sweetness of the corn will vary, so add salt to taste.

Char the tortillas on an open gas flame (or on the grill) until they start to char in several places.

Scoop the corn mixture into a tortilla and serve with scallions and cilantro.

Summertime Chilaquiles

We grow a big garden every year. Wait, I should rephrase that: my husband maintains a garden every year, and my daughter and I pluck a few weeds and turn the compost pile a handful of times in exchange for homegrown produce. It's a sweet deal.

My husband starts in the winter, plotting out his bed shapes, and he even brings the compost bins into the garage to keep them going when it's too cold outside. I like to think that he's fueled by the thought of enjoying these chilaquiles with summer veggies.

If you've never had chilaquiles, they're leftover tortillas (or tortilla chips) stirred into a spicy red sauce (mine is mild) with cheese and sometimes chorizo. There are many variations.

My variation uses black beans instead of chorizo, the last of the tortilla chips from the bag, and the sauce from the Lentil Enchiladas on page 157. In fact, if I'm making enchiladas, I make a double batch of sauce with these chilaquiles in mind for a future meal.

This is a classic breakfast or brunch dish, but it makes a great dinner, too. Other variations I've had and loved: "soyrizo" or chorizo instead of black beans, fried eggs on top, cotija instead of goat cheese, and a "zero veggies" version (which, admittedly, is much more traditional).

10 ounces Homemade Enchilada Sauce (page 159)

1 tablespoon neutral oil

1 ear fresh corn, shucked, silks removed, and sliced off the cob (see Note)

1 small zucchini, sliced

1 small red bell pepper, sliced into thin strips

4 big handfuls corn tortilla chips

1 cup cooked black beans (about ½ can, drained and rinsed)

8 cherry tomatoes, halved, for garnish

2 ounces goat cheese, crumbled, for garnish

Cilantro, for garnish

Pickled red onions, for garnish

Prepare the enchilada sauce as directed on page 159.

In an 8-inch skillet, heat the oil over medium-high heat.

Add the corn to the skillet and cook without stirring often until it starts to blacken in places.

Next, stir in the zucchini and bell peppers. Cook until softened and golden brown.

Scrape the veggies out of the skillet and onto a plate.

Place the skillet back on the heat (no need to clean it) and pour in the enchilada sauce. Bring the sauce to a simmer and then start adding handfuls of tortilla chips, stirring between each addition.

When the skillet is almost full of the chips, stir it gently to coat every chip in the sauce.

Add the veggies back to the skillet along with the black beans and heat through.

Place the skillet directly on the table (use an oven mitt!) and sprinkle the tomatoes, crumbled goat cheese, cilantro, and pickled onions on top. Dig in!

NOTE: You may substitute ½ cup of frozen roasted corn. Add it to the skillet frozen after cooking the zucchini and pepper.

Steak for Two with Scalloped Potatoes

When my husband and I cook together in the kitchen, I love to put him in charge of the meat while I focus on a rich, cheesy, carb-laden side dish. My scalloped potatoes for two are the perfect accompaniment to any steak dinner. Steak is actually a super quick dinner to make! And it's almost entirely hands-off.

My version of steak requires just a few minutes of hands-on time and a quick trip to the oven. I use filet mignon for this special occasion recipe, and I love that the small portion size leaves extra room for more scalloped potatoes.

2 filet mignon steaks, about
   6 ounces each
Salt
Freshly ground black pepper
1 tablespoon neutral oil
1 sprig fresh rosemary
Scalloped Potatoes, for serving
   (recipe follows)

Remove the steaks from their packaging, and allow them to rest at room temperature for 30 minutes. Flip after 15 minutes.

Meanwhile, preheat the oven to 425°F and ensure the middle rack is in place.

Press a generous amount of salt and pepper into all sides of the steaks.

In a medium skillet with an oven-safe handle (no nonstick pans here, please), heat the oil over high heat. It's ready when it's too hot to hold your hand 3 inches over the pan for 3 seconds.

Place the steaks in the pan. Don't touch or move them while they sear, 5 minutes. Use tongs to gently turn the steaks over. Add the rosemary sprig to the pan, pushing it around in the pan juices a bit, and then immediately move the skillet to the preheated oven.

Continue to cook the steaks in the oven, 5 minutes for rare, and up to 9 minutes for medium to well done. When the steaks come out of the oven, move them to a plate, tent the plate with foil, and let them rest for 5 minutes.

Serve the steaks with any accumulated juices drizzled on top and with scalloped potatoes on the side.

Scalloped Potatoes

Scalloped potatoes are a labor-of-love for me. They require a sauce made on the stovetop and then a long bake in the oven. I take my scalloped potatoes over the top with fried onions. They are great with steaks but also work as a vegetarian dinner with a good salad.

Olive oil cooking spray

10 ounces baby Yukon gold potatoes (about 4 small ones)

1 tablespoon unsalted butter

2 tablespoons flour

1 cup half-and-half

¾ teaspoon salt

¼ teaspoon freshly ground black pepper

½ cup sharp Cheddar, plus extra for topping

¼ cup diced onion

2 tablespoons fried onions (such as French's)

Preheat the oven to 350°F.

Lightly spray two mini cast-iron dishes that measure about 5 inches in diameter with cooking spray.

Thinly slice the potatoes in ⅛- to ¼-inch slices. (There's no need to peel the potatoes).

Meanwhile, in a small saucepan over medium heat, melt the butter. Whisk in the flour, followed by the half-and-half.

Whisk until the mixture thickens and coats the back of a spoon. Stir in the salt, pepper, and Cheddar.

Turn off the heat and stir until the Cheddar completely melts into the cheese sauce. It will be a thick sauce.

Spread 1 tablespoon of the cheese sauce in the bottom of each cast-iron skillet. Layer one-quarter of the sliced potatoes in each skillet.

Next, spread one-quarter of the cheese sauce in each skillet (using a little less than half of the cheese sauce). Sprinkle 1 tablespoon of diced onions over each skillet.

Repeat: Use the last of the sliced potatoes, all but a few tablespoons of the cheese sauce, and the last of the diced onions.

Scrape the last few tablespoons of the cheese sauce on top, and then sprinkle the fried onions and extra grated Cheddar over everything.

Bake for 30 minutes.

Cranberry Balsamic Chicken Skillet

The dreaded leftover cranberry sauce from Thanksgiving and Easter (we serve it with ham on Easter) is something my husband and I look forward to now that this recipe is in our lives.

One of the reasons I love bone-in, skin-on chicken thighs is because they typically come four to a package, which is perfectly portioned for two people! If you're new to bone-in chicken thighs, I think you'll find they have much more flavor than chicken breasts. The dark meat has a richer flavor that stands up to this punchy cranberry sauce.

1 tablespoon neutral oil

Salt

Freshly ground black pepper

4 bone-in, skin-on chicken thighs, trimmed of any excess fat

1 cup chicken broth

1 cup leftover cranberry sauce (you can use canned, jellied, whole berry sauce)

2 tablespoons balsamic vinegar

2 sprigs fresh rosemary

Buttered egg noodles or brown rice, for serving

In a 10-inch skillet, add the oil and turn the heat to medium-high.

Meanwhile, season both sides of the chicken thighs very well with salt and pepper.

When the oil is shimmering, add the chicken pieces, skin side down.

Don't move the chicken until it browns thoroughly and releases from the pan easily, about 7 to 9 minutes.

Meanwhile, whisk together the chicken broth, cranberry sauce, and balsamic vinegar.

When the first side is golden brown, flip the chicken and cook on the other side. Add the cranberry mixture to the pan after flipping.

Nestle the fresh rosemary in the sauce.

Turn the heat down to medium and cook the chicken, uncovered, until it registers 165°F in the thickest part of the thigh. The sauce will thicken as the chicken cooks.

Serve the chicken with the cranberry sauce on top. I like to serve this chicken with egg noodles or buttered brown rice.

French Lentils and Kielbasa

I made a version of this dinner when I first started cooking for myself. My family's background is Czech, and so I grew up around my fair share of kielbasa. When I saw a kielbasa and lentil salad mixture in an issue of *Fine Cooking*, I made it immediately because I had always been curious about French lentil salads. I definitely didn't grow up with them!

This salad became an obsession of mine that hasn't wavered in over a decade. I make it at least twice a month, and I purposely seek out French lentils for it.

The right kind of lentils (French lentils, or du Puy lentils) hold their shape when cooked, unlike the more common types of lentils that have a tendency to dissolve into a mushy mess. When the lentils are hot, they're tossed with a bright vinaigrette, which they soak up so nicely. The fried kielbasa pieces are the perfect counterpart to vinegary, herby lentils.

FOR THE LENTILS

1 cup French (du Puy) lentils

2 sprigs fresh thyme (a big pinch of dried thyme works here, too)

2 bay leaves

1 garlic clove, smashed

½ small onion, whole

1 small carrot, split lengthwise

½ teaspoon freshly ground black pepper

½ teaspoon salt

½ package of kielbasa

Vinaigrette (recipe follows)

First, cook the lentils: Combine the lentils, herbs, garlic, onion, carrot, salt, and pepper in a 2-quart saucepan with a tight-fitting lid. Add enough water to cover the lentils by 2 inches. Bring the mixture to a gentle simmer and cook, partially covered, for about 25 to 35 minutes or until the lentils are tender. Check on the lentils periodically to make sure there's enough water in the pan; add extra water if the lentils absorb it all.

Next, slice the kielbasa into ½-inch slices and add them to a dry skillet over medium heat. Sauté the kielbasa pieces until the edges start to turn golden brown, then remove them from the skillet and set aside.

(continued)

2 tablespoons red wine vinegar

1 teaspoon Dijon mustard

¼ teaspoon salt

¼ teaspoon freshly ground
   black pepper

3½ tablespoons walnut oil

Chopped fresh parsley, for
   garnish

Sliced scallions, for garnish

While the kielbasa is cooking, make the vinaigrette by whisking together the vinegar, mustard, salt, and pepper in your serving bowl. Slowly drizzle the walnut oil in while whisking constantly to emulsify the vinaigrette.

When the lentils are tender, drain them, and then immediately add them to the bowl with the vinaigrette. Toss to coat. Add the parsley and scallions. Stir in the kielbasa and serve.

Baked Greek Shrimp

When we cook together in the kitchen, we typically divide and conquer—one person does prep, the other person mans the pan. But with a one-pan meal like this, there's not much for the other person to do except keep the wine glasses full.

2 teaspoons olive oil

½ small yellow onion, diced

1 garlic clove, minced

1¼ cups tomato purée (or canned crushed tomatoes)

¼ cup dry white wine

¼ teaspoon salt

¼ teaspoon freshly ground black pepper

½ pound raw shrimp, peeled and deveined with tails left on

⅓ cup crumbled feta cheese

2 tablespoons chopped fresh parsley

2 tablespoons fresh oregano leaves

Crusty French bread, for serving

Preheat the oven to 425°F.

In an 8-inch skillet, heat the olive oil over medium heat.

Stir in the diced onion, garlic, tomato puree, wine, salt, and pepper. Bring to a gentle simmer and cook for about 5 minutes.

Next, nestle the shrimp all around the pan with the tails sticking up. Sprinkle the feta evenly on top.

Bake the skillet for about 12 minutes, until the shrimp are pink and cooked through.

Before serving, sprinkle the fresh parsley and oregano on top.

Serve with crusty French bread.

Chicken Parmesan Meatballs

The flavors of chicken Parmesan are too good not to stuff into a meatball skillet and enjoy. This skillet dinner is much easier to make than traditional chicken Parmesan because you don't have to serve it with spaghetti. If your partner is having a "fitness journey moment" and watching their carbs, they will love this! Just leave the bread off their plate and don't mention the bread crumbs in the meatballs.

⅓ cup panko bread crumbs

2 tablespoons grated Parmesan

8 large fresh basil leaves, chopped

½ teaspoon salt

¼ teaspoon freshly ground black pepper

½ teaspoon dried Italian seasoning

½ small yellow onion, minced

1 garlic clove, minced

1 large egg

½ pound lean ground chicken

1 tablespoon olive oil

One 16-ounce jar marinara sauce

1 cup shredded mozzarella

Crusty French bread, for serving

Preheat the oven to 400°F.

In a small bowl, mix together the bread crumbs, Parmesan, chopped basil, salt, pepper, Italian seasoning, onion, garlic, and egg. Mix it together very well, and then stir in the chicken lightly. The meatball mixture should be homogenous, but try not to overmix it.

Press the mixture flat into the bowl as best as you can, and divide it in half by eye. Make four meatballs from each half of the mixture.

In a small, oven-safe skillet, heat the olive oil over medium-high heat. Sear the meatballs in the skillet until the outside is golden brown, but don't worry about cooking the meatballs through at this point.

Once the meatballs are evenly browned on all sides, gently pour the marinara sauce into the skillet.

Top with the shredded mozzarella, and slide the skillet in the oven for 10 minutes. Test a meatball to make sure it's done before serving with crusty bread.

Creamy Mushroom Chicken Skillet

I created this recipe when we were craving one of those saucy little chicken dinners that you can almost always find on a restaurant menu these days. I frequently order any dish that consists of chicken, mushrooms, and cream sauce.

I've served this over buttered egg noodles or Really Good Mashed Potatoes (page 227). I call for thin-cut chicken breasts, but if your store doesn't carry them, slice one regular large chicken breast in half like a book to get two cutlets for this recipe.

1½ tablespoons unsalted butter
2 teaspoons olive oil
¼ cup all-purpose flour
¼ teaspoon salt
Freshly ground black pepper
2 thin-cut chicken breasts
Half an 8-ounce box of sliced
   cremini mushrooms (or 7
   whole mushrooms, sliced)
1 garlic clove, minced
½ cup dry white wine
⅓ cup heavy cream
¼ cup grated Parmesan
¼ cup oil-packed sun-dried
   tomatoes, drained

In an 8-inch skillet, melt the butter and olive oil over medium heat.

Meanwhile, sprinkle the flour on a small plate and add a generous pinch of salt and pepper to it. Stir it gently with a fork to combine. Dredge each chicken cutlet in the flour, evenly coating both sides, and then place it in the skillet.

Cook the chicken until it's golden brown on the first side (about 4 to 5 minutes), then flip and cook the other side until golden brown. Remove the chicken from the skillet (don't worry if it's not cooked all the way through at this point).

Now add the mushrooms to the skillet and sauté until they soften and release their juices, about 5 minutes. Add the garlic to the skillet and cook for 30 seconds.

Pour the wine, heavy cream, Parmesan, and sun-dried tomatoes over the mushrooms and nestle the chicken breasts back into the skillet.

Let the mixture simmer and cook the chicken breasts all the way through, about 5 minutes longer. Sprinkle the Parmesan and sun-dried tomatoes on top before serving.

Sloppy Joe Tater Tot Skillet

The beauty of a good sloppy joe is in the tangy-sweet tomato sauce. This skillet meal is my regular craving. I think it's because the flavors of the sweet and tangy sauce conjure up my strong feelings about barbecue sauces from the Carolinas. There's nothing not to love about a good, tangy sauce!

The other beauty of this sloppy joe recipe is the hidden veggies. I feel better about eating my half-skillet portion because of the onion, tomatoes, and bell pepper in the sauce.

1 tablespoon unsalted butter

½ onion, diced

½ small yellow bell pepper, diced

2 garlic cloves, minced

½ pound ground turkey

One 8-ounce can tomato sauce

¼ cup ketchup

2 tablespoons brown sugar

1 tablespoon Worcestershire sauce

¼ teaspoon garlic powder

¼ teaspoon onion powder

2 tablespoons yellow mustard

½ teaspoon salt

Freshly ground black pepper

Half a 1-pound package frozen tater tots

Preheat the oven to 450°F.

In a small skillet (8- or 10-inch), melt the butter over medium heat.

Add the diced onions and bell pepper to the skillet and cook for about 5 minutes to soften. Lower the heat if the onions start to brown.

Next, add the garlic and cook for 30 seconds.

Add the ground turkey to the skillet and cook while breaking it up with a wooden spoon. Cook until the turkey is no longer pink.

Add all the remaining ingredients to the pan (except the tater tots). Bring the mixture to a simmer and cook for about 3 minutes.

Next, scatter the tater tots over the surface of the skillet and slide the pan in the oven to bake for about 17 minutes, until the tater tots are golden brown and cooked through.

NOTE: I top this sloppy joe skillet with tater tots, because I can almost never get through a package of hamburger buns without some mold (living in a small-batch house means most bread gets moldy before it gets used!). However, if you're up for it, I have a recipe for small-batch Brioche-Style Hamburger Buns on page 260, and they're perfect with this recipe.

Egg Roll in a Bowl

Too often, date night becomes takeout night in our house. So, I'm committing to making our own takeout at home—together!

The flavors are bright and fresh, and yes, they taste exactly like the inside of an egg roll! I like to add a handful of chow mein noodles that I have leftover from the Crunchiest Chinese Chicken Salad (page 136) for some crunch factor.

This is one dinner that we never get tired of, plus all the cabbage makes me feel virtuous!

2 teaspoons neutral oil

2 garlic cloves, minced

2 scallions, white and green parts sliced separately

One 1-inch piece fresh ginger, grated

½ pound ground pork

2 cups shredded Napa cabbage leaves

1 carrot, grated

2 teaspoons sesame oil

Handful fresh cilantro leaves, for serving

2 teaspoons sesame seeds, for serving

2 big handfuls chow mein noodles, for serving

In an 8-inch nonstick skillet, heat the neutral oil over medium-high heat.

Add the garlic, the white part of the scallions, and the ginger, and sauté for about 30 seconds, until very fragrant.

Add the ground pork to the pan and cook while breaking it up with a spoon. Cook until almost all of the pink has cooked out.

Add the shredded cabbage, grated carrots, sesame oil, and the green parts of the scallions, and cook until the cabbage just begins to start wilting, about 3 to 4 minutes.

Divide the mixture between two bowls and serve with the cilantro, sesame seeds, and chow mein noodles sprinkled on top.

Chicken Sausage with Orzo and Broccolini

I rely on this dinner often, especially when we're running late-afternoon errands or getting home late from work. I always keep chicken sausage in the freezer because it defrosts rather quickly. I grab the box of orzo from my pantry and broccolini (or any other type of green vegetable) from the fridge. You can use frozen broccoli florets here, too! The sun-dried tomatoes in oil are a nice touch, but feel free to skip them if you're in a hurry.

I didn't call for any salt in this recipe because the sausage, broth, and Parmesan bring so much salt to the table. Taste before serving and make sure you're happy with it.

Another note: I reach for a cooked chicken sausage product that has savory flavors in it, often labeled "Italian style." While chicken-apple sausage is the easiest to find, I don't love the sweet apples in this recipe. Find a great savory chicken sausage that you like—even better if it's spicy!

1 tablespoon olive oil

2 links cooked chicken sausage (Italian-style; about 6 ounces), sliced into coins

¾ cup orzo pasta

2 cups chicken broth

1 garlic clove, minced

1 small bunch broccolini, trimmed (or 1½ cups frozen broccoli florets)

¼ cup oil-packed sun-dried tomatoes, drained

Freshly ground black pepper

3 tablespoons grated Parmesan, for serving

In an 8-inch nonstick skillet, heat the olive oil over medium heat.

Add the sliced sausage to the skillet and cook until the edges start to brown, about 3 to 4 minutes, stirring often.

Next, add the orzo pasta and cook while stirring for 3 minutes, until some of the orzo starts to brown.

Add the broth and minced garlic and bring the mixture to a boil. Gently lay the broccolini on top, then cover the skillet.

Reduce the heat to medium-low and cook until the pasta is al dente and has absorbed most of the liquid, about 13 minutes.

Stir in the sun-dried tomatoes, grind black pepper on top, and serve with Parmesan at the table.

CHAPTER 3.
SMALL POTS OF SOUP

A big pot of soup is delicious on day one, but how do you feel about it on day seven of leftovers? My first foray into scaling down recipes began with soup—a pot of minestrone, to be exact. I love soup and could happily eat it as my main meal most nights of the week. But even a soup lover needs variation and I welcome smaller batch recipes of the classics: Beef Bourguignon, Zuppa Toscana, and an authentic Texas Tortilla Soup. Plus, you'll love my method to make either minestrone or ribollita, depending on what you have in your pantry. Get ready to put the soup on!

Easiest Tortellini Soup for the Busiest Nights

I have all of the ingredients to make this soup on hand at all times. It's easy because most everything lives in the freezer: frozen cheese tortellini, frozen peas, jars of homemade chicken stock from another day, and cubes of basil pesto from the summer harvest. I add a handful of baby spinach to the bottom of the bowl before serving if I have it; if not, the soup is delicious without it. Serve with grated Parmesan and an excess of freshly ground black pepper.

4 cups chicken stock

10 ounces cheese tortellini (not defrosted, if frozen)

1 cup frozen peas

¼ cup basil pesto

2 big handfuls fresh baby spinach

Salt

Freshly ground black pepper

Grated Parmesan, for serving (optional)

In a small stock pot, bring the chicken stock to a boil.

Drop in the tortellini and cook according to the package directions (about 4 minutes, or until they're all floating).

Turn off the heat and stir in the peas and pesto.

Taste the soup and add salt and freshly ground black pepper to taste.

In the bottom of two serving bowls, add the baby spinach. Ladle the soup over the spinach and serve with Parmesan at the table, if using.

NOTE: If you don't have chicken stock on hand, I recommend the jars of stock base. They keep nearly forever in the fridge, and all you have to do is add water.

Beef Bourguignon

While this French beef stew is admittedly a lot of work for a small pot, after one bite you will agree it's worth it. Once you sear the onions and cook them in beef broth until it's thick and syrupy, you'll vow to make this at least once a month. The deliciousness that is seared baby onions with thyme sprigs and reduced beef broth will make your partner proclaim that it's last-meal-on-earth worthy; it's first-date-worthy; it's Valentine's Day worthy! I'm speaking from experience here.

It bakes for 2 hours in the oven, but you can absolutely do it the day before. I actually recommend cooking it the day before and letting it rest in the fridge overnight. The flavors bloom overnight, plus you can skim off any fat before reheating and serving.

I serve it over Really Good Mashed Potatoes (page 227), but buttered egg noodles are also amazing.

FOR THE STEW

3 ounces bacon (about 3 slices), chopped

½ pound beef stew meat (chuck or round)

1 carrot, sliced into 1-inch chunks

½ red onion, sliced

1 tablespoon all-purpose flour

1 cup red wine

¾ cup beef broth

3 fresh thyme sprigs

1 bay leaf

1 garlic clove, crushed

Salt

Freshly cracked black pepper

Preheat the oven to 325°F.

In a 3.5-quart mini cast-iron pot, add the chopped bacon. Turn the heat to medium and cook the bacon, occasionally stirring, until it's no longer pink and is starting to crisp up. Remove it from the pan with a slotted spoon, leaving the bacon grease in the pan. Set it aside.

Generously sprinkle salt and pepper over the beef chunks, then add them to the pan from which you just removed the bacon. Sear the beef on all sides until it's golden brown (but don't worry about cooking it through).

Add the sliced carrot and red onion to the pan. Cook for 3 to 5 minutes, stirring occasionally.

Sprinkle the flour over the vegetables and meat and cook for 1 minute while stirring.

Add the wine, beef broth, thyme sprigs, bay leaf, and garlic clove to the pan. Add the bacon pieces and a final big pinch of salt and pepper.

(continued)

6 ounces baby onions (about
   1 dozen)

1 tablespoon unsalted butter

1 tablespoon olive oil

¼ cup beef broth

1 bay leaf

1 thyme sprig

FOR THE MUSHROOMS

12 button mushrooms,
   quartered

½ tablespoon olive oil

1 tablespoon unsalted butter

Place the lid on the pot and move it to the oven. Cook for 2 hours, stirring after 1 hour.

After 1 hour, peel the baby onions and slice off the root ends.

Place the whole onions in an 8-inch skillet with the butter and olive oil. Turn the heat to medium-high and sear the onions until they start to caramelize in a few places, about 5 to 6 minutes.

Add the beef broth, bay leaf, thyme sprig, and a big pinch of salt and pepper to the skillet. Lower the heat to medium-low and cook until the beef broth reduces to a syrupy liquid and the onions are meltingly soft, about 10 to 15 minutes.

Pour the onion mixture into a bowl.

Without wiping out the pan, add the mushrooms, olive oil, and butter. Turn the heat to medium and cook until the mushrooms are starting to caramelize around the edges, about 7 to 8 minutes. Remove the mushrooms from the pan and add them to the bowl with the onions.

When the beef is done cooking in the oven, remove the lid to stir in the onions and mushrooms.

Serve the stew over Really Good Mashed Potatoes (page 227) or hot, buttered egg noodles.

Tortilla Soup

I'm from Texas, so you can trust this recipe!

I will bet that my recipe for tortilla soup is different from anything you've ever had at a restaurant, and more authentic, too. I scaled down the recipe from Cheryl Jamison's cookbook, which is a book I turn to when I want to cook something authentically Tex-Mex or Mexican for company. For me, her recipes are a taste of Texas on each plate (or in each bowl), and I would have been lost without them all the years I lived outside of my home state.

I'm happily back to living in Texas and still making this recipe as often as I like.

4 cups beef broth

½ yellow onion, sliced into half-moons

3 whole garlic cloves, skin left on

1 tablespoon neutral oil

1 cup canned crushed tomatoes (or sauce, whatever you have)

½ teaspoon dried oregano

1 tablespoon chopped canned chipotles

Juice of 1 lime

2 corn tortillas, sliced into 1-inch strips

½ cup shredded, cooked chicken

First, bring the beef broth to a boil in a small soup pot. Boil it for about 15 to 30 minutes to reduce it to roughly 3 cups of liquid.

Meanwhile, preheat the oven broiler to high. Toss the onions and whole garlic cloves with the oil. Spread evenly on a large baking sheet and broil until the onions are dark golden brown in places and the garlic skin is golden brown, too. It will take about 5 to 8 minutes.

Remove the onions and garlic from the oven and let them cool. Once cooled, remove the paper skins from the garlic and dice it roughly.

Stir the onions, garlic, and all the remaining ingredients (except the lime juice) into the reduced beef broth. Bring it to a gentle simmer and cook for 10 minutes.

Add the lime juice, taste, and then adjust for salt. I don't call for salt in the recipe, because the beef broth can vary a lot in saltiness, and I like when the lime provides the majority of the "salty" flavor. But you might like a little salt, so add it if you feel it needs it.

Divide between two bowls to serve.

Minestrone/Ribollita

While pretending a recipe for minestrone soup is interchangeable with a recipe for ribollita (an Italian soup with tomatoes, kale, and stale bread cubes) will make some Italians run for the Alps, I had to do it.

The truth is, I love the herby flavors of minestrone soup so much, but I also frequently have leftover bread in my house. So, when I have leftover stale bread to use up, I make ribollita. When I don't, I toss in a small pasta (like ditalini) to make minestrone. They're both fantastic.

The thing that sets great minestrone apart from good minestrone is fresh rosemary. So use a 4-inch fresh sprig if you have it.

1 tablespoon olive oil

½ small onion, diced

1 stalk celery, diced

1 small carrot, diced

1 garlic clove, minced

1 small zucchini, halved and sliced

2¾ cups vegetable broth

One 14-ounce can crushed tomatoes

1 cup cooked kidney beans

½ teaspoon dried oregano

1 teaspoon dried parsley

¼ teaspoon dried basil

¼ teaspoon dried thyme

One 4-inch sprig fresh rosemary

¾ teaspoon salt

¼ teaspoon freshly ground black pepper

½ cup ditalini pasta (or ½ cup stale bread cubes for ribollita version)

1 cup loosely packed baby kale

¼ cup Parmesan, plus extra

In a 3.5-quart mini Dutch oven, heat the olive oil over medium-high heat.

Add the diced onion, celery, and carrot. Cook for 3 to 4 minutes, until the onion is translucent.

Add the garlic and zucchini, and cook for 30 seconds.

Stir in the vegetable broth, tomatoes, and kidney beans. Add all of the herbs, salt, and pepper, then bring the mixture to a boil.

Add the ditalini and cook until it's done, about 8 minutes. If you're using stale bread instead, stir it in, then bring the mixture to a gentle simmer cook for about 5 minutes.

Add the kale and Parmesan just before serving.

Golden Cauliflower Soup with Saffron and Harissa

I've been eating this saffron-infused cauliflower soup since high school. Growing up, my Persian friends frequently invited me to dinner at their houses, and I was soon enveloped by the new-to-me flavors of saffron, barberries, and hot black tea with sugar cubes.

Tasting chicken that had soaked in a saffron yogurt marinade all day and been grilled until charred in several places, served with huge pans of *tahdig* (also called stuck-pot rice), forever changed me.

When I first tasted this fragrant cauliflower soup, I was amazed. I'd never seen a broth so golden yellow, and I'd never tasted something so simple that was so good. Sautéing the onions in butter until they're softened—but never browned—gives the soup a depth of flavor.

Today, I puree the soup and add a splash of *harissa* (a hot chili pepper paste from North Africa) on top. A few torn Castelvetrano olives on top mimic the vinegary bite of *torshi* (Persian pickled vegetables) that were usually served on the side.

2 cups chicken broth

⅛ teaspoon saffron threads (0.025 grams)

3 tablespoons butter

2 cups diced onions

1½ pounds cauliflower

Salt

Harissa, for serving

Castelvetrano olives, pitted, for serving

In a small Dutch oven, add 2 cups of water and the chicken broth and bring to a simmer.

Remove from the heat and add the saffron. Cover and let it steep for 20 minutes.

Meanwhile, in a large skillet, melt the butter over medium heat. Add the onions and cook until softened and translucent (making sure not to let them brown around the edges), about 15 minutes, while stirring frequently.

Once the saffron is done blooming in the broth, add the cauliflower to the pot and stir in the cooked onions.

Bring the pot to a simmer and cook until the cauliflower is tender.

Using an immersion blender (or transferring the soup to a blender carefully), puree the soup until it's smooth. If you're using a regular blender, crack the lid so steam can escape while blending.

Taste the mixture and add salt to taste. The flavor of the cauliflower should be the first thing you taste, followed by a saffron finish. Add salt until the flavors are balanced.

Divide between two serving bowls and swirl some harissa paste on top of each, followed by a few chopped Castelvetrano olives.

Zuppa Toscana

I've got a thing for this rich Italian soup, but, as expected, I have opinions about it. Zuppa Toscana should be very creamy without being thick, the potatoes should have their skins, and freshly ground black pepper should be on the table for serving.

It's warm, comforting, and everything you need for dragging hunks of bread through with each bite.

2 slices bacon, chopped

2 Italian sausage links, removed from casing (or ½ pound bulk Italian sausage)

1 small onion, diced

Pinch of red pepper flakes

2 cups chicken broth

½ teaspoon salt, plus more to taste

1 large russet potato, cut in half and then sliced into ¼-inch half-moon shapes

1 cup packed chopped kale

½ cup heavy cream (or half-and-half)

Freshly ground black pepper

In a mini Dutch oven or saucepan, add the chopped bacon. Turn the heat to medium and cook the bacon while occasionally stirring until it begins to crisp up around the edges.

Remove the bacon from the pan, leaving the drippings behind.

Next, add the sausage, diced onion, and red pepper flakes to the pan and cook while breaking up the sausage with a wooden spoon.

Once the sausage is beginning to brown around the edges and is mostly done, add the chicken broth, salt, and potato slices.

Cover the pan and bring it to a gentle simmer to cook the potatoes for about 8 to 10 minutes.

Once the potatoes are tender, add the kale and cover the pan again for 3 minutes to cook the kale.

Turn off the heat and stir in the heavy cream. Taste the soup and add freshly ground black pepper and additional salt to taste.

Ladle into two bowls and top with the chopped bacon.

CHAPTER 4.
BOWLS OF COMFORT

Truthfully, my favorite recipes are tucked into this chapter. It's hard to believe such big flavor can be found in a single bowl, but layers of texture, complimentary spices, and plenty of easy, one-bowl sauces make every recipe here sing. Please don't miss the recipe for Black Bean Lasagna Bowls—it's unbelievably delicious and crave-worthy! I rounded out my collection of bowl recipes with a few salads that were created with the guidance of my very talented chef friend. She changed my mind on salads as comfort food, and who knew the secret lies in the dressing? Bowl recipes are great to scale up and be used as lunch the next day, so when you find one that you like, double it!

Black Bean Lasagna Bowls

The deliciousness of these lasagna bowls blows my mind every time I make them. This recipe has such a short ingredient list that I always think I'm leaving something out. The chipotles and apple cider vinegar are the secret ingredients here that bring so much flavor!

6 ounces short pasta (such as ziti or penne)

One 14-ounce can crushed tomatoes

¼ teaspoon ground cumin

¼ teaspoon salt

1 tablespoon chopped chipotles in adobo sauce

¾ teaspoon apple cider vinegar

1½ cups black beans

1 cup ricotta (store-bought or homemade on page 41)

2 tablespoons sour cream

¼ teaspoon salt

Cilantro, for garnish

Pickled onions, for garnish

Bring a large pot of salted water to a boil. Cook the pasta according to the package directions and drain.

Meanwhile, combine the tomatoes, cumin, salt, chipotles, and vinegar in a small saucepan with a lid. Bring the mixture to a gentle simmer and let it cook for about 15 minutes.

Stir in the black beans and remove from the heat.

In a small bowl, whisk together the ricotta, sour cream, and salt. Set aside.

Stir the drained pasta into the tomato mixture.

Serve with dollops of the ricotta and garnish with pickled onions and cilantro.

Almost Korean Beef Bowls

With these saucy little beef bowls, I'm sharing a recipe for pickled carrots that you will want to keep in your fridge at all times. Pickled carrots give this rice bowl a little punch, and after you enjoy them here you'll find all sorts of uses for them.

While these bowls aren't authentically Korean bulgogi, the flavor reminds me of bulgogi with its spicy, sweet, and salty sauce. The ponzu marinade doubles as a beef marinade and Brussels sprout sauce, saving tons of prep time.

If ponzu sauce is new to you, think of it as soy sauce with a citrus and bonito kick. If you can't find ponzo, use soy sauce with a bit of lemon zest grated in.

FOR THE PICKLED CARROTS

¾ cup rice wine vinegar

¼ cup granulated sugar

½ teaspoon ground coriander

3 medium carrots

FOR THE RICE

½ cup white rice

1 cup water

FOR THE SAUCE

¼ cup ponzu sauce

2 tablespoons rice wine vinegar

1 tablespoon toasted sesame oil

Juice of 1 lime

¼ teaspoon cayenne pepper

FOR THE REST

½ pound thin beef strips (often called "stir-fry cut.")

1 tablespoon neutral oil

½ pound Brussels sprouts

Sesame seeds, for garnish

First, make the pickled carrots. Combine the rice wine vinegar, sugar, and coriander in a quart mason jar and shake to dissolve.

Next, scrub the carrots very well, and then use a vegetable peeler to make ribbons by shaving down each side of the carrot.

Place the carrot ribbons into the mason jar, give it a gentle shake to combine, and then let the carrots sit for at least 1 hour before using.

Carrots keep for several weeks in the fridge.

Make the rice by combining it with 1 cup of water in a small saucepan with a tight-fitting lid. Let the rice and water come to a boil, lower the heat, cover, and cook for about 18 minutes, until the water is absorbed and the rice is fluffy.

Meanwhile, make the ponzu marinade: Combine the ponzu, vinegar, sesame oil, lime juice, and cayenne pepper in a small bowl. Pour half of this mixture over the beef in a small bowl to marinate, and reserve the remaining half.

Wash and trim the Brussels sprouts of their bases and any outer leaves that don't look great.

In a large skillet, preferably cast-iron, heat the neutral oil over high heat. When the oil is shimmering and very hot, add the Brussels sprouts in one even layer. Sear the sprouts on one side until golden brown, flip, and then push them to the edges of the pan.

In the middle of the pan, add the beef with the marinade mixture. Toss it in the pan while it cooks; it will be cooked through in about 2 minutes or less!

Turn off the heat, pour in the remaining ponzu marinade, and stir to coat everything with the sauce.

Divide the rice between each bowl and add Brussels sprouts and beef on top. Serve with pickled carrots and a sprinkling of sesame seeds.

Falafel Bowls

After many years as a vegetarian, I found myself at the bottom of a long list of people who have been disappointed by bad falafel. Just because it's a fried falafel, doesn't mean it's a good one. Not all fried foods are created equally.

These falafels are the furthest thing from the dry, boring, and mealy ones you may have had before. They're crispy on the outside, soft on the inside, and full of so much herby flavor. The garlic-yogurt dip on the side is what elevates this to a meal that I could eat every summer day for the rest of my life!

FOR THE FALAFEL

1¾ cups cooked chickpeas (see Note) or one 15-ounce can, rinsed and drained

Juice of 1 lemon

3 scallions, root ends removed

1 garlic clove, grated on a microplane

½ cup packed cilantro (stems and leaves)

½ cup packed parsley (stems and leaves)

1 large egg

½ teaspoon salt

½ teaspoon freshly ground black pepper

½ teaspoon ground cumin

½ teaspoon smoked paprika

½ cup olive oil, for frying

FOR THE DIP

½ cup Greek yogurt

½ small cucumber, grated

1 garlic clove, grated on a microplane

¼ teaspoon salt

Freshly ground black pepper

FOR THE REST

1 cup cherry tomatoes, sliced

Pita bread, for serving

1 small cucumber (plus the rest of the one you used for the dip), sliced

A few mint leaves, torn

In the bowl of a food processor, combine all of the falafel ingredients except the olive oil.

Pulse until everything is combined and the herbs are tiny flecks throughout the batter.

Meanwhile, heat the olive oil in a nonstick pan over medium-high heat.

Using a cookie scoop, scoop out portions of the batter and drop them in the olive oil. Fry the falafels on one side until golden brown, then flip and repeat. When both sides are golden brown, roll the falafel in the pan for a few more minutes to make the edges golden brown.

You'll get about a dozen small falafels.

Remove the falafels from the oil and let them cool on a paper towel–lined plate.

Next, whisk together all of the dip ingredients. Taste and adjust for salt and pepper.

Divide the tomatoes, pita, cucumber slices, and mint leaves between two bowls. Top with the falafel and the dip to serve.

NOTE: I soak ½ cup dry chickpeas overnight, and then cook them in my Instant Pot for 10 minutes on high pressure. Add 1 tablespoon of salt to the water after they've cooked, and let them soak for about 20 minutes. Drain before using.

Greek Bowls

This recipe is a little bit of everything I love in one bowl, with an extra dose of protein because of the quinoa tabbouleh.

It's a dish that often comes together naturally for me since I almost always have quinoa in the pantry, chicken in the freezer, a container of store-bought hummus, and feta cheese in the fridge. The sharp, briny flavors of this bowl will make you want to double the recipe to have leftovers for an easy make-ahead lunch for the next day!

FOR THE QUINOA TABBOULEH

1 cup chicken broth

½ cup dry quinoa

3 tablespoons lemon juice

½ teaspoon dried oregano

2 garlic cloves, minced

2 tablespoons olive oil

FOR THE CHICKEN

¼ pound (about 3 or 4) chicken tenders, cut into 1-inch pieces

Salt

Freshly ground black pepper

½ teaspoon dried oregano

1 tablespoon olive oil

FOR THE TOMATO SALAD

¾ cup sliced cherry tomatoes

¼ cup chopped fresh parsley

2 tablespoons chopped fresh mint

½ small red onion, thinly sliced

1 small Persian cucumber, chopped

¼ cup pitted Kalamata olives

FOR SERVING

Store-bought hummus

⅓ cup crumbled feta cheese

In a small saucepan with a tight-fitting lid, bring the chicken broth to a boil. Add the quinoa, reduce the heat to low, and cover. Cook for about 15 minutes or until most of the liquid is absorbed and the quinoa is done (the little curly tail will come out of the grain when it's done).

Let the quinoa cool slightly while you whisk together the dressing. In a small bowl, combine the lemon juice, oregano, and garlic. Add the olive oil slowly while whisking to emulsify the dressing.

Pour the dressing over the hot quinoa and stir to coat. Set aside.

Meanwhile, combine the chicken with a generous pinch of salt, a few grinds of black pepper, oregano, and olive oil. Mix very well.

Preheat a nonstick skillet. When it's hot, add the chicken pieces and cook while stirring once or twice until done, about 10 minutes. Remove from the skillet and set aside.

Next, assemble the salad: Combine the cherry tomatoes, parsley, mint, red onion, cucumber, and olives. (If raw onions are a bit strong for you, then soak the thinly sliced pieces in ice-cold water for about 15 minutes. Drain, then add to the salad.)

To serve, divide the quinoa into each bowl, then divide the chicken between each bowl, too. Evenly distribute the tomato salad mixture and put a dollop of hummus in each bowl before topping with the crumbled feta.

Steak and Sweet Potato Bowls with Creamy Kale

Admittedly, this is a weird recipe for kale salad. It probably sounds like it's missing an ingredient, like oil or something, but it's not. And please don't think I'm kidding when the recipe instructs you to massage the kale salad. The best kale to use for this is Lacinato or dinosaur kale—it's super dark green, almost bluish, and when massaged it has aromas of banana and coconut. I'm not crazy, try it!

The kale is simply mashed with avocado, the juice of half a lemon, and cayenne pepper (as much as you can handle). Yes, that's it!

Roasted sweet potatoes and expertly seared steak tips go on top for a super hearty yet healthy meal. This isn't your average kale salad!

You can make the sweet potatoes ahead of time (or use some leftover ones you already have, and marinate the steak tips the night before, too.

2 small sweet potatoes

½ pound steak tips

¼ cup soy sauce

Zest and juice of ½ lemon

¼ teaspoon freshly ground black pepper

¼ teaspoon ground coriander

1 tablespoon neutral oil

1 small bunch (or 4 big handfuls) Lacinato kale, washed and destemmed

1 small avocado, pit removed

Cayenne pepper (start with ¼ teaspoon and work your way up, to taste)

First, preheat the oven to 375°F and line a small baking sheet with foil for easy cleanup.

Prick the sweet potatoes all over with a fork and roast until tender (the skin will start to wrinkle slightly), about 40 minutes. Test the sweet potatoes with a fork to ensure they're soft all the way through. The part of the sweet potato touching the pan will brown, and some sweet sugars might bubble out—this is sweet potato perfection!

Meanwhile, chop the steak tips into ½-inch pieces.

In a bowl, combine the soy sauce, lemon zest, pepper, coriander, and oil. Whisk well.

Add the steak tips and let them marinate for 15 minutes or overnight.

Heat a large skillet (preferably cast-iron) over high heat. Remove the steak tips from the marinade and place them in the skillet when it is nice and hot.

(continued)

Cook the steak on each side until golden brown, about 8 to 10 minutes in total.

When the steak is done, move it to a plate to cool slightly.

Next, make the kale salad. After removing the stems, chop the kale into bite-size pieces.

Place the kale in a big bowl and add the avocado, lemon juice, and ¼ teaspoon of the cayenne pepper. Use your hands to smoosh it all together. Really get in there and massage it for at least 3 minutes. The avocado will melt and form the dressing with the lemon juice. Taste and add more cayenne pepper, if you like.

To assemble the salad, peel and slice the sweet potatoes. Toss them in the bowl with the kale. Add the steak tips and toss everything together to combine.

Divide between two bowls and serve.

Coconut Curry Noodle Bowls

We've moved a lot over the past six years (four states, to be exact), and the first thing I do is make sure my new grocery store carries our favorite curry paste.

A little bowl of curry is so comforting to us when we find ourselves in a new home. If I have my beloved jar of curry paste and a can of coconut milk in the pantry, I can almost always turn the contents of my vegetable drawer into these curry noodle bowls. Vary the vegetables by the season and serve it with extra fish sauce on the table.

4 ounces (2 bundles) rice noodles (also called stir-fry noodles)

Half a 14-ounce block extra firm tofu

2 tablespoons coconut oil

2 tablespoons red curry paste

One 1-inch piece fresh ginger, grated on a microplane

1 can light coconut milk

7 stalks fresh asparagus, tough ends removed and sliced into 1-inch pieces

1 carrot, peeled and thinly sliced

Handful sugar snap peas

2 tablespoons soy sauce

1 tablespoon rice wine vinegar

1 tablespoon fish sauce

Cilantro, for serving

Lime wedges, for serving

First, bring a large kettle of water to a boil. Place the rice noodles in a large bowl. Pour the boiling water on top, cover with a dinnerplate, and set aside.

Next, chop the tofu into bite-size cubes.

Heat the coconut oil in a large nonstick skillet. Make sure the oil coats the entire bottom of the pan; if it doesn't, add more oil.

Add the tofu cubes to the pan and cook on one side, without disturbing, until golden brown. Stir and continue to cook until all sides are golden brown, about 10 minutes.

Remove the tofu from the pan and let it drain on a paper towel–lined plate.

Add the curry paste and grated ginger to the skillet and cook for about 30 seconds while stirring to loosen it up and flavor the oil.

Next, stir in the coconut milk and bring it to a gentle simmer.

Add the sliced asparagus, carrots, sugar snap peas, soy sauce, and rice wine vinegar.

Stir and let the mixture simmer until the vegetables are tender, about 8 to 10 minutes. Stir in the fish sauce.

Finally, drain the noodles and add them to the skillet. Toss everything together.

Divide the mixture between two bowls and serve with the fried tofu cubes on top. Garnish with cilantro and lime wedges.

Peanut Lime Noodle Bowls

This is the first-ever dinner I made for my daughter that made her pause and say, "Mmm, Mama, this is good!" She was almost two years old, and when someone that young (and incapable of lying) tells me a recipe is good, I take note.
I guess I should have known, because what kid doesn't love peanut butter?

FOR THE BOWLS

6 ounces soba noodles (or your favorite kind of noodle)

1 small bell pepper

1 small carrot

½ cup frozen edamame

½ cup frozen corn (or 1 cob with kernels sliced off)

1 scallion, green part chopped

Fresh cilantro, for serving

PEANUT LIME BLACK PEPPER SAUCE

¼ cup creamy peanut butter

1 tablespoon fresh lime juice

1 tablespoon soy sauce

Smallest pinch of cayenne pepper

3 tablespoons neutral oil

1 teaspoon sesame oil

2½ teaspoons freshly ground black pepper

Grated fresh ginger, about ¼ teaspoon (optional)

Bring a large pot of salted water to a boil. Cook the soba noodles according to the package directions.

When the soba noodles are almost done cooking, add the frozen edamame and corn to the pot, just to defrost and cook them through, about 60 seconds.

Meanwhile, remove the stem and seeds from the bell pepper and slice it into thin strips. Peel and slice the carrot into thin strips, too.

Drain the noodles and vegetables and run them under cold water to cool everything down.

Next, whisk together all the ingredients for the peanut lime sauce with 3 tablespoons hot water. Taste and adjust salt and pepper.

Toss the noodles, veggies, and peanut sauce together and serve with chopped scallions and fresh cilantro.

Chicken Burrito Bowls

This is one of the most requested dinners for two in my house. I frequently double the ingredients to have on hand for Friday night dinners, when I'm most prone to stopping by the burrito bowl place—you know the one.

The secret to ultra-creamy guacamole for topping these bowls is mayo. If you're morally opposed to mayo in guacamole (hi, Mom), mash your avocado with lime juice instead.

I use brown rice to keep things slightly healthier, but feel free to use white rice and cut your cook time in half.

FOR THE RICE

½ cup brown rice

¼ teaspoon salt

Juice of ½ lime

Small handful chopped cilantro

FOR THE CHICKEN

1 tablespoon tomato paste

¼ teaspoon ground cumin

¼ teaspoon chili powder

¼ teaspoon garlic powder

¼ teaspoon salt

¼ teaspoon freshly ground
   black pepper

Juice of ½ lime

1 tablespoon olive oil

½ pound chicken tenders
   (about 4 tenders), or 1 boneless,
   skinless chicken breast

¼ cup frozen corn

½ red bell pepper, thinly sliced

1 small onion, thinly sliced

¼ teaspoon salt

¼ teaspoon freshly ground
   black pepper

½ cup cooked black beans

First, get the rice going because it takes the longest. Combine the brown rice and 1 cup water in a 1-quart saucepan. Bring it to a boil, turn the heat to low, cover, and cook for 35 to 40 minutes, until all of the liquid is absorbed by the rice.

When the rice is done, stir in the salt, lime juice, and chopped cilantro. Set it aside, covered, to keep warm.

Next, prepare the chicken: Whisk together the tomato paste, cumin, chili powder, garlic powder, salt, pepper, and lime juice. Use kitchen scissors to cut the chicken into bite-size chunks. Add the chicken to the marinade and let it marinate in the fridge for at least 20 minutes or up to a few hours ahead of time.

Preheat a large skillet over medium-high heat and add the olive oil. Lightly drain the chicken from the marinade and sear it in the skillet until golden brown on all sides, about 7 to 10 minutes. Check to ensure the chicken is done before removing it from the skillet.

After removing the chicken from the skillet, add the corn, bell pepper, onion, salt, and pepper. Cook while stirring occasionally, about 10 minutes, or until the veggies are softened and starting to turn golden brown on the edges. Turn off the heat and stir in the beans. Set it aside.

FOR THE GUACAMOLE (IF YOU'RE A GUAC-ON-TOP PERSON)

1 avocado

1 tablespoon mayonnaise

Pinch of salt

Freshly ground black pepper

To make the guacamole, mash the avocado together with the mayonnaise, salt, and pepper.

To serve, divide the rice between two bowls. Add the chicken, veggies, beans, and guacamole on top.

Smoky Pork and Yellow Rice Paella Bowls

I came up with these pork bowls one night when I was craving the flavors of paella. The pork is coated in smoked paprika, orange zest, and orange juice (a greater combination there never was), and the smoky tomato sauce on top is the perfect partner to the saffron rice. I love the smoky tomato sauce so much that I often double it and use it on shredded chicken later in the week. You can make the tomato sauce ahead of time and marinate the pork the night before, too.

FOR THE PORK

½ pound pork tenderloin

Zest and juice of ½ navel orange

2 teaspoons smoked paprika

1 garlic clove, minced

1 tablespoon olive oil (for cooking)

Tomato sauce (recipe follows)

FOR THE RICE

½ cup long-grain white rice, rinsed

Generous pinch of saffron (about 40 threads)

½ cup frozen peas

Small handful chopped green olives

Fresh parsley, for serving (optional)

First, marinate the pork: Dice the pork into 1-inch chunks. Sprinkle the orange zest, orange juice, smoked paprika, and garlic on top. Toss to coat well. Marinate in the fridge for at least 20 minutes and up to overnight. You can make your tomato sauce ahead of time, or while you cook the rice and pork.

When you're ready to eat, make the rice. In a 2-quart saucepan with a lid, combine the rinsed rice with 1 cup of water. Bring it to a boil, lower the heat to low, cover, and cook for 18 minutes.

When the rice has about 5 minutes of cooking time left, bloom the saffron in 2 tablespoons of warm water.

When the rice is done, remove the lid, stir in the saffron water and frozen peas, then cover and let it rest while you cook the pork.

Heat a medium skillet (preferably cast-iron) over high heat. Once hot, add the olive oil, followed by the pork pieces. Sear the pork on all sides until golden brown, about 3 minutes a side. Move the cooked pork to a plate to cool slightly.

To serve, divide the rice between two bowls and top with the pork, tomato sauce, chopped green olives, and parsley.

FOR THE TOMATO SAUCE

2 tablespoons olive oil

½ small onion, diced

2 garlic cloves , minced

1 cup crushed tomatoes

1 teaspoon smoked paprika

Pinch of red pepper flakes

½ teaspoon salt

To make the sauce, add the olive oil to a small saucepan and heat over medium heat. Add the diced onion and sauté until softened, about 4 to 5 minutes.

Next, add the garlic and cook for 30 seconds.

Stir in the crushed tomatoes, smoked paprika, red pepper flakes, and salt.

Simmer the mixture for 10 to 15 minutes.

Taste it and adjust the seasonings to your liking.

Roasted Potato Bowls with Broccoli and Gribiche

My palate leans toward bold flavors—like briny cornichons and Dijon mustard—and *sauce gribiche* is something I often crave. It's a punchy combination of mayonnaise, egg yolks, and Dijon mustard with capers and cornichons. It's bright, tangy, and assertive. This bowl tastes best at room temperature.

FOR THE BOWLS

1 pound baby Yukon gold potatoes
2 tablespoons neutral oil
Salt
Freshly ground black pepper
2 large eggs
2 cups broccoli florets

FOR THE SAUCE GRIBICHE

¼ teaspoon salt
1 tablespoon Dijon mustard
2 teaspoons white wine vinegar
1 tablespoon olive oil
1 tablespoon capers
2 cornichons, finely chopped
Freshly ground black pepper
2 tablespoons chopped fresh parsley

Preheat the oven to 400°F.

Scrub the baby potatoes and slice them in half. Spread the potatoes evenly on a large baking sheet and drizzle with the oil. Toss to coat.

Sprinkle a generous amount of salt and freshly ground black pepper over the potatoes and toss.

Roast the potatoes until they're done, about 20 to 25 minutes. Let them cool slightly.

Meanwhile, hard-boil the eggs: Place the eggs in a small saucepan and cover them with water. Bring to a boil and, once boiling, cover and turn off the heat. Let the eggs sit for your desired level of doneness (up to 9 minutes for hard-boiled and as little as 5 minutes for a soft yolk).

After cooking immediately rinse the eggs under cold running water, peel them, and set them aside.

Rinse out the pot from boiling the eggs and bring about ½ cup of water to a boil in it. Once boiling, add the broccoli florets, turn the heat off, cover, and let it sit for about 5 minutes, until the broccoli is crisp-tender and bright green. Drain and set aside.

Make the sauce gribiche: Whisk together all the ingredients and taste to adjust for seasoning. Sometimes I add more vinegar or more olive oil to make the sauce thinner.

To serve, pile the roasted potatoes, steamed broccoli, and chopped eggs into two bowls. Drizzle the sauce gribiche on top and serve.

Crunchiest Chinese Chicken Salad

Sometimes a big bowl of the crunchiest salad ever is just the thing on a hot summer night. The bright, zingy flavors of this salad are so refreshing and satisfying that it almost feels like a cool breeze.

I suggest starting with 1 teaspoon of freshly grated ginger and working your way up to my preferred amount of 1 tablespoon. Fresh ginger gives this dressing its spicy punch.

The dressing doubles as the chicken marinade here if you want to bake the chicken, but when I'm in a hurry I use leftover rotisserie chicken or I poach the chicken in the Instant Pot. Both methods create a bowl piled high with crunchy cabbage, crisp veggies, and a bold vinaigrette to make the crunchiest salad ever.

1 large chicken breast

1½ cups chicken broth

2 large Napa cabbage leaves

1 small red bell pepper

½ cup frozen edamame

1 small carrot

2 scallions

¼ cup slivered almonds

½ cup cooked chow mein
noodles

FOR THE DRESSING

2 tablespoons rice wine
vinegar

2 teaspoons toasted sesame oil

2 teaspoons soy sauce

2 teaspoons coconut sugar

1 to 3 teaspoons freshly grated
ginger root

First, decide how you will cook the chicken. You have two options:

You can double the dressing ingredients, toss the chicken in it as a marinade, and bake at 350°F until it's done (about 35 minutes).

Or you can place the chicken in the bottom of your Instant Pot Mini and add chicken broth until it's almost submerged. Place the lid on the Instant Pot, turn the valve to "Seal," and cook on high pressure for 10 minutes with a forced pressure release when the timer is up.

While the chicken cooks, thinly slice the cabbage. Deseed and remove the stem from the bell pepper before slicing it into thin strips, then set it aside. Peel and grate the carrot and set it aside. Slice the scallions thinly and set them aside.

Bring a small pot of water to boil and cook the edamame according to the package directions; drain and rinse under cold water until cool. Set them aside.

When the chicken is done, shred it with two forks.

Divide the cabbage, bell pepper, edamame, carrot, and scallions between two bowls.

Next, whisk together all of the dressing ingredients. Start with 1 teaspoon of fresh ginger, taste, and add more if desired.

To serve the salad, place the chicken over each salad bowl, drizzle on the dressing, and sprinkle with almonds and chow mein noodles before tossing and serving.

Roasted Mushroom, Barley, and Brie Bowls

This is my quick little go-to dinner for two when I find leftover roasted veggies in the fridge from my Butter-Roasted Vegetables escapades (page 185). I prefer mushrooms for this, but honestly, any leftover vegetable will work!

This recipe is quick because I use pearled barley that cooks in just 10 minutes. Follow the directions on your bag of barley for the best results. And always cook it in chicken broth for extra flavor.

¾ cup pearled barley

2¾ cups chicken broth

Pinch of salt, plus more to taste

1 cup butter-roasted mushrooms (page 188)

2 tablespoons unsalted butter

½ cup chopped Brie chunks

3 sprigs fresh thyme

Freshly ground black pepper, to taste

In a small saucepan with a lid, combine the barley and chicken broth with a pinch of salt.

Cook the barley according to the package directions. After about 10 minutes, stir the pot and taste. Continue cooking, adding water, if the barley isn't done at this point. The barley should absorb nearly all of the chicken broth.

When the barley is done, turn off the heat and add the leftover mushrooms to the pan. Place the lid on to warm them through.

Finally, stir in the chopped Brie, the leaves from the thyme sprigs, and salt and pepper to taste.

Corn, Tomato, and Dill Summer Pasta Salad

I have this sweet friend named Sherrie Castellano who makes the most incredible salads and soups. She hosts pop-up dinners regularly, and while we eagerly await each course, I'm most excited for her salad and soup courses.

The first time she served me a salad, I was awe-struck. She has a special skill for properly seasoning it and making it taste like a homogenous dish instead of a pile of greens with some "stuff" on it. I'm not sure if this makes sense, but when you eat Sherrie's salads, you taste one harmonious flavor, not all the individual parts. Her soups are incredible blends with just the right amount of crunch on top.

Since I'm lucky enough to call her a real-life friend, I get to stand in the kitchen next to her sometimes while she makes salads, and I've learned a thing or two from Sherrie: taste and add salt until it tastes right to you—until it sings with one harmonious flavor.

Also, she taught me to celebrate vegetables in every way: the raw form, the cooked version, and the way they play with herbs. This salad has raw corn for sweetness, cherry tomatoes for acidity, and fresh dill to play with the vegetables. I think it goes without saying that seasonal, local corn and tomatoes are the only way to go for this recipe, right?

I love giant pearl couscous for its slippery mouthfeel, but you can use any type of small pasta you prefer.

1 cup pearl couscous

3 tablespoons high-quality apple cider vinegar

¼ teaspoon salt

⅛ teaspoon freshly ground black pepper

3 tablespoons olive oil

1 cup sliced local cherry tomatoes

1 raw corn ear, kernels shaved off

3 tablespoons fresh chopped dill

Cook the couscous in plenty of salted water, according to the package directions. Drain and rinse lightly with cool water. Set aside.

In the bottom of a serving bowl, whisk the vinegar, salt, and pepper together. Slowly stream in the olive oil while continuing to whisk to make an emulsified dressing.

Add the couscous to the bowl with the dressing and toss. Stir in the sliced tomatoes and raw corn kernels. Stir in the dill very thoroughly, then taste. Add additional salt until it tastes right to you.

Peach Cucumber Salad with Fresh Mozzarella

Once I mastered the perfect apple cider vinaigrette for the Corn, Tomato, and Dill Summer Pasta Salad (page 141), which has a higher proportion of vinegar than a regular vinaigrette, any and all summer salads were fair game.

The only way—and I really mean the only way—that this salad works is with the ripest summer peach. Luckily, cucumber season overlaps peach season, so the two are fit to be paired.

The addition of pearls of mozzarella is my attempt to make a meal out of this salad. Torn pieces of fresh mozzarella are great here, too, or burrata if you prefer.

3 tablespoons high-quality apple cider vinegar

¼ teaspoon salt, plus more to taste

⅛ teaspoon freshly ground black pepper, plus more to taste

3 tablespoons extra virgin olive oil

1 ripe summer peach

1 small cucumber (Persian cucumbers are ideal here)

½ cup fresh mozzarella pearls (or torn pieces)

10 fresh mint leaves

In a large serving bowl, whisk the vinegar, salt, and pepper together. Slowly stream in the olive oil while continuing to whisk to make an emulsified dressing.

Next, pit the peach and thinly slice it (leaving the skin on). Set aside.

Scrub the cucumber very well and, using a vegetable peeler, shave it into ribbons.

Pile the cucumber ribbons and thinly sliced peaches into the bowl with the dressing and toss gently.

Add the fresh mozzarella, followed by a good pinch of salt and an extra grinding of black pepper.

Using your fingers, tear the mint leaves into the bowl and toss very well to combine everything.

Make a mini bite with a bit of everything in the bowl, taste, and adjust for seasoning—vinegar and black pepper make this salad sing.

CHAPTER 5.
LOVE FROM THE OVEN

This collection of baked dinners for two are mostly hands-off and perfect for days when you need to get a few things done while dinner is cooking. I've included my two favorite marinades to use on any type of protein you may have. I've committed them both to memory and they pop into my mind every time I see a block of tofu, a few chicken breasts, or half of a cut of beef in my freezer. This chapter also contains my favorite method for making side dishes to accompany any of the meals in this book. Endlessly adaptable and simple, these veggies will grace your table more frequently now, I promise!

Fish en Papillote

Everything about this recipe name sounds fancy, but it couldn't be easier or quicker. It involves finding a great piece of fish, a simple, super flavorful rub, and a seasonal vegetable. In the first few days of spring, this amounts to the first of the season's cod, red curry paste, a splash of coconut milk, and a tangle of asparagus spears.

The best way to fold the parchment paper closed is to fold it on top of itself as you go around. So, once you make the initial fold, make sure the next fold includes a bit of the first fold. And so on. It will stay closed without any additional pinning.

1 tablespoon butter

½ pound fresh asparagus, ends trimmed

10 sprigs cilantro

Two 6-ounce pieces cod

2 tablespoons red curry paste

Salt

¼ cup canned full-fat coconut milk

Preheat the oven to 400°F.

Have ready two large squares of parchment paper (that measure roughly 12 inches) to give you plenty of room to crimp it closed.

Cut the butter in half and place one piece slightly to the right of center on each piece of parchment paper. Divide and pile the asparagus and cilantro sprigs on top of the butter.

Rub each piece of cod thoroughly with the red curry paste and place them on top of the asparagus and cilantro sprigs. Sprinkle salt over the top.

Lightly crimp the parchment paper up enough so you can pour the coconut milk on top of each piece of fish without it spilling out, then begin your real crimping process.

To crimp the packets closed: Start by folding the parchment paper like a book—pull the left side of the parchment paper toward the right, over the fish bundle. Then, from the top, begin crimping by folding the paper twice on top of itself, and then gather the next bit of paper to crimp, incorporating the previous fold while you go. Move down the edge of the paper; when you get to the end, it should hold itself closed, but if not, tuck the end piece underneath.

Bake for about 15 minutes and serve quickly.

NOTE: Feel free to swap out the cod for whatever type of fish you like, the coconut milk for a dry white wine, and the asparagus for whatever is fresh at the farmers' market. Other delicious combos:

    2 salmon fillets + 3 tablespoons dry white wine + 1 cup cherry tomatoes
    2 halibut fillets + 2 tablespoons butter + ½ lemon, sliced
    2 sea bass fillets + 3 tablespoons vermouth + handful olives and cherry tomatoes

Oven Risotto with Crispy Kale

Hands-free risotto with a healthy side dish that cooks at the same time is my definition of a great date-night dinner for two. If you love creamy risotto at a restaurant but don't want to stand at the stove and stir it for 20-plus minutes, try this oven-baked version.

While it may sound crazy (or virtuous?) to call for a full ½ pound of kale to serve two people, it's actually because the kale shrinks so much as it cooks in the oven.

A creamy bowl of risotto with crisp kale chips on top is a perfect Meatless Monday meal or date-night dinner for two.

1 tablespoon olive oil

¼ small yellow onion, minced

1 garlic clove, minced

¾ cup Arborio rice

½ cup dry white wine

Freshly ground black pepper

¼ teaspoon salt

1½ cups chicken stock

2 tablespoons unsalted butter, divided

¼ cup grated Parmesan

FOR THE KALE

8 ounces kale, chopped

1 tablespoon olive oil

Salt

Freshly ground black pepper

Preheat the oven to 350°F.

In a small Dutch oven, heat the olive oil over medium-high heat. Add the diced onion and cook until translucent, about 5 minutes, while stirring occasionally.

Add the minced garlic to the pan and cook until fragrant, about 30 seconds.

Next, add the rice and cook for about 3 minutes, until the edges are starting to become a touch translucent.

Add all of the wine and continue to cook while stirring occasionally until it's mostly absorbed, about 5 minutes.

Finally, stir in the chicken stock. Place the lid on the pan and place the pan on the middle rack in the oven. Bake for 30 minutes, stirring once at 15 minutes.

Meanwhile, toss the chopped kale with the olive oil, season with salt and pepper, and spread it in one even layer on a large baking sheet. Place the sheet in the oven after the rice has been in for 10 minutes. The kale only takes 20 minutes total—check on it after 10 minutes and stir. Continue to roast until the kale crisps and begins to turn golden brown around the edges. When the kale is done, remove the tray from the oven and allow it to cool on the pan.

When the risotto is done, after 30 minutes, carefully remove the pan from the oven, remove the lid, and stir in the butter and Parmesan.

Divide the risotto between two bowls and top each with a generous handful of crispy kale.

Barbecue Chicken–Stuffed Sweet Potatoes

If you don't count yourself among the sweet potato fan base, this recipe is equally good with russet potatoes. I've been known to double or triple this recipe and use a mix of both.

   As a Texan, I'll try not to lecture you too much about your barbecue sauce choices, but if your favorite barbecue sauce is very dark brown and contains molasses, you might find it a touch too sweet for this recipe. If you're looking for the right sauce to use with this recipe, it's a tangy vinegar-based barbecue sauce. I'm a Stubb's or Dreamland sauce girl myself, but really, use what you like. I won't judge (too much).

2 medium sweet potatoes

1 cup shredded cooked chicken

½ cup barbecue sauce

½ cup shredded smoked Gouda

Chopped red onions, for
   garnish

Cilantro leaves, for garnish

Preheat the oven to 400°F. Scrub the sweet potatoes and prick holes in the skins with a fork.

Place the potatoes on a foil-lined baking sheet and bake for about 40 minutes. If you insert a knife all the way through, there will be no resistance. Let the potatoes cool but leave the oven on.

In a small bowl, stir together the chicken, barbecue sauce, and Gouda.

When the potatoes are cool enough to handle, slice them open. Push both ends toward the middle to make the potato open like a bowl.

Using a spoon, scoop out the sweet potato flesh, leaving about a ½-inch border to keep its shape.

Stir the sweet potato flesh into the bowl with the chicken mixture.

Finally, divide the chicken mixture in half and stuff it back into each of the sweet potato skins.

Place the stuffed potatoes back on the baking sheet and return them to the oven just until the cheese melts and everything heats through, about 10 minutes.

Serve garnished with chopped red onion and cilantro.

Carrot Ginger Salmon

I'll never tire of ways to get salmon on the table quickly. If you've ever had carrot-ginger dressing on a salad, you'll recognize it here with a bit more heat from the ginger. Double it and keep it on hand for salads and any other protein during the week.

FOR THE SALMON

Two 6-ounce salmon fillets

2 teaspoons olive oil

Salt

Freshly ground black pepper

FOR THE CARROT-GINGER SAUCE

¼ cup rice wine vinegar

¼ cup neutral oil

1 large carrot (slightly more than ½ cup sliced)

¼ cup peeled fresh ginger coins

1 tablespoon lemon juice

1 tablespoon honey

¼ teaspoon salt

Preheat the oven to 425°F and line a sheet pan with parchment paper.

Drizzle the olive oil over the salmon fillet and sprinkle evenly with salt and pepper.

Slide the pan into the hot oven and roast for 10 minutes. Check the salmon to see if it's done; if it's thick, it might take up to 4 more minutes in the oven.

Meanwhile, add all the ingredients for the carrot-ginger sauce to a high-speed blender. Blend on high until the mixture turns into a sauce. If you don't have a high-speed blender, you might have to add a splash of water to get it going in a regular blender or food processor.

Taste the dressing and add additional salt or honey, if needed.

When the salmon is done, move it to a serving plate and serve with bowls of the carrot-ginger sauce for enjoying.

Puff Pastry Veggie Tart

This puff pastry tart serves two purposes: to feature a vibrant pesto—either your favorite store-bought jar, my pepita cilantro pesto (page 175), or my spinach pesto (page 34)—and to enjoy buttery puff pastry. We love to pile on our favorite garden veggies and rarely make this the same way twice.

While you can definitely use garden tomatoes in this tart, I find that tomato season overlaps with the hottest time of the year (a.k.a. when I never want to turn my oven on), so I typically make this veggie tart in the fall with the last of the zucchini and thyme before the frost.

You can use any veggies you like here, but I highly recommend including mushrooms for their meaty flavor!

1 sheet frozen puff pastry, defrosted on the counter for 20 minutes

¼ cup pesto

⅓ cup Boursin cheese (any garlic-herb cheese works)

3 to 4 mushrooms, sliced

1 small zucchini, cut into sticks

½ onion, sliced

Fresh thyme sprigs

First, preheat the oven to 400°F.

Remove the puff pastry sheet from the box, and gently unfold it onto a parchment paper–lined baking sheet.

Using a rolling pin, gently roll out the sheet until it's about ½ inch larger on all sides.

Using a fork, prick the dough all over, leaving a ½-inch border around the edges.

Next, dollop the pesto on top of the dough and spread it over the dough, stopping about ½ inch from the edge.

Crumble the Boursin cheese and scatter it evenly across the pesto.

Arrange the mushrooms, zucchini, onion, and thyme sprigs over the cheese.

Bake for 30 to 35 minutes, until the crust is golden brown and the edges of the tart are puffed.

Serve immediately.

Lentil Enchiladas

I survived on lentil enchiladas my freshman year of college. I was newly vegetarian (like any good college kid), and the vegetarian section of the food hall always had lentil enchiladas. They were cheesy, satisfying, and full of protein.

I like to think my version exceeds the school lunch option, and judging by how enthusiastically these get eaten in our house, I think I'm right.

This seems like a lot of ingredients, but stay with me—you're mostly just making lentils taste like meat in the best way possible. This is a great recipe to make together in the kitchen: have one person measure and the other person stir.

Makes 6 enchiladas

¾ cup green lentils

1 tablespoon neutral oil

1 tablespoon chili powder

2 teaspoons ground cumin

½ teaspoon smoked paprika

½ teaspoon salt

¾ teaspoon freshly ground
   black pepper

½ teaspoon garlic powder

½ teaspoon onion powder

½ teaspoon dried oregano

Red pepper flakes (optional)

¼ red onion, diced

1 tablespoon tomato paste

10 ounces Homemade
   Enchilada Sauce (recipe
   follows)

First, add the lentils to a small saucepan with 1¼ cups of water. Add a generous pinch of salt. Bring the mixture to a boil and cook, stirring occasionally, until the lentils absorb all of the water and are tender. If they absorb the water before they are tender, add more water, but try to add as little as possible.

When the lentils are done, remove them from the pan. Add the oil and all of the herbs and spices to the pan.

Cook the herbs and spices over medium heat until fragrant, about 1 minute.

Add the diced onion and cook until softened, about 3 to 4 minutes.

Add the lentils back to the pan along with the tomato paste. Stir until everything is combined.

Remove the lentil mixture from the heat.

Preheat the oven to 350°F.

(continued)

FOR THE ENCHILADAS

6 flour tortillas (about 6 to 8
  inches in diameter)
2 cups shredded Colby-Jack
Avocados, for serving
Pickled onions (page 116), for
  serving
Cilantro, for serving

Prepare the enchilada sauce.

Once the sauce is done, pour half of it into a small baking dish (mine is 6-by-9 inches, but anything that will hold your tortillas will work).

Lay each tortilla flat and fill with one-sixth of the filling mixture. Add a small handful of cheese on top and roll it up.

Place it seam-side down in the baking dish.

Repeat with the remaining tortillas.

Pour the remaining enchilada sauce on top, then top with the rest of the cheese.

Bake until the enchiladas are golden brown and bubbling, about 20 minutes.

To serve, top with avocados, pickled onions, and cilantro.

Homemade Enchilada Sauce

Makes 10 ounces

2 tablespoons unsalted butter

2 tablespoons neutral oil

3 tablespoons all-purpose flour

2 tablespoons tomato paste

2 heaped tablespoons chili
  powder

½ teaspoon ground cumin

½ teaspoon ground onion

¼ teaspoon garlic powder

¼ teaspoon salt

¼ teaspoon freshly ground
  black pepper

Pinch of cayenne pepper

2 cups beef stock

2 teaspoons apple cider
  vinegar

In a 2-quart saucepan, melt the butter and oil over medium heat.

Whisk in the flour and cook until it turns a light golden color, about 4 minutes.

Whisk in the tomato paste and all of the spices. Cook for 1 minute until fragrant.

Slowly pour in the beef stock and bring to a simmer. Let the mixture simmer for 5 minutes to thicken.

Remove the sauce from the heat and stir in the vinegar.

NOTE: You can use chicken stock instead of beef stock, if you prefer.

Mini Quiche Lorraine with Salad (and the Only Salad Dressing You'll Ever Need)

Let me say first that I'm not a big egg person. I will eat them when made for me, and I make them frequently for my family. So, for the most part, I've avoided quiche. The version of quiche most commonly found is little more than scrambled eggs with vegetables stirred in, similar to a frittata. It lacks the creamy, silky consistency of a proper quiche, made the French way.

Quiche Lorraine is something I fell in love with at a small proper French bakery called Nathaniel Reid Bakery in St. Louis. After one bite, I knew exactly what all other quiche recipes were missing.

I scale down my favorite recipe for Quiche Lorraine here and bake it in six muffin cups. It's a great dinner for two with a side salad, and they're even great reheated in the oven the next morning.

You can use store-bought tart shells here if you like; omit the prebaking in that case and fill the shells with the custard mixture and bake as directed.

Makes 6 mini quiches

FOR THE PASTRY SHELLS

½ cup flour plus 2 tablespoons

⅛ teaspoon salt

6 tablespoons (3 ounces) unsalted butter, diced and kept cold

1 large egg yolk, beaten

First, make the pastry: In a medium bowl, whisk together the flour and salt. Add the cold butter and work it through the flour using a pastry blender, two knives, or your fingertips. Work the butter into the dough until a few marble-size pieces of butter remain—leaving chunks of butter is what makes puff pastry puff, unlike piecrust, which has smaller pieces of butter throughout.

Add 1 tablespoon of ice water and stir lightly with a fork. Does the dough come together easily, or are there dry crumbs on the bottom? If so, add 1 tablespoon of ice water. Add a third tablespoon of ice water if the dough needs it to come together.

(continued)

2 slices bacon, sliced into
   1-inch pieces

½ small onion, sliced (you can
   also use leftover caramelized
   onions instead from page 46)

½ cup half-and-half

¼ teaspoon salt

⅛ teaspoon freshly ground
   black pepper

⅛ teaspoon freshly grated
   nutmeg (optional)

2 tablespoons grated Parmesan

Salad dressing (recipe follows)

Lettuce, for serving

Scoop the dough out of the bowl and place it on a floured surface.

Roll the dough away from you into a thin rectangle shape, fold it in thirds like a letter, turn it 90 degrees, and repeat. Do this six times, flouring the surface and rolling pin each time to prevent sticking.

Fold the dough up like a letter one final time, then wrap it in plastic wrap and place it in the fridge for at least 20 minutes, or up to 2 days.

Next, make the filling: Add the bacon pieces to a small skillet. Turn the heat to medium and fry the bacon until it starts to crisp. Remove the bacon from the pan with a slotted spoon and set it aside.

With the heat still on, add the onion slices and cook until they're golden brown and caramelized. You can also use any leftover caramelized onions.

Remove the onions from the skillet.

In a small bowl, whisk together the half-and-half, salt, pepper, nutmeg, and grated cheese. Set this aside with the bacon and onion for later.

Preheat the oven to 400°F.

Once the dough is done chilling, unwrap it, flour your counter, and roll it into a 12-by-9-inch rectangle. Using a knife, cut it into six equal pieces.

Grease a six-well muffin pan and gently lay a dough piece in each cup. Press it down lightly, making sure there is plenty of dough overhanging the edges of each cup.

Prick the bottom of the tart shells very well with a fork.

Brush the egg yolk over the tart shells, and bake them for 10 minutes.

(continued)

After 10 minutes, remove the tarts from the oven. Sprinkle the bacon and onions in each tart (saving some for the top), and then divide the custard mixture between the cups. Top the custard with a few pieces of bacon and a few strands of caramelized onion.

Bake for 10 to 11 minutes more, keeping an eye on the tarts so the edges don't get too brown.

Let the tarts cool for 5 minutes, then remove them from the pan and serve warm.

The Only Salad Dressing You'll Ever Need

1 tablespoon balsamic vinegar
1 tablespoon extra virgin olive oil
½ teaspoon salt
½ teaspoon dried oregano
¼ teaspoon onion powder
⅛ teaspoon garlic powder
¼ teaspoon freshly ground black pepper
⅓ cup plain yogurt (Greek is fine, but regular is better)

In a small bowl, combine all the ingredients and whisk to dissolve the spices.

Toss the dressing with 3 cups of mixed greens and serve with the quiches.

Crispy Pork Chops with Asparagus and Lemon Cream

This hearty "fried" pork chop that comes with a rich, creamy lemon sauce is a perfect hands-free dinner for two. It all bakes on the same sheet in the oven!

While I usually reach for the pencil-thin asparagus spears, the best asparagus to use here is the slightly thicker stalks so that they cook in the same amount of time as the pork chops.

FOR THE PORK CHOPS

1 cup panko bread crumbs

Big pinch of salt

Freshly ground black pepper

1 large egg

2 boneless pork chops, about
    1 inch thick

Olive oil cooking spray

½ pound thick asparagus
    spears

1 tablespoon olive oil

FOR THE LEMON CREAM SAUCE

½ cup heavy cream

1 tablespoon cornstarch

Zest and juice of 1 lemon

¼ teaspoon salt

Freshly ground black pepper

1 tablespoon grated Parmesan

Preheat the oven to 400°F. Have a large sheet pan lined with parchment paper ready.

In a shallow bowl, add the bread crumbs, a big pinch of salt, and plenty of freshly ground black pepper.

In another shallow bowl, whisk the egg with a splash of water.

Next, dunk the pork chops in the egg, followed by the bread crumb mixture. Use your fingers to press the bread crumbs into the pork very well to make a thick coating.

Place the pork chops on the sheet pan.

Arrange the asparagus spears around the pork and toss with the olive oil.

Spray the pork chops with cooking spray before sliding them into the oven to bake. At 15 minutes, check the temperature of the pork. If it is at least 140°F, remove it from the oven and allow it to rest for a few minutes to climb up to the proper temperature of 145°F. If not, slide it back into the oven for another 3 to 5 minutes.

(continued)

In a microwave-safe glass measuring cup, whisk together the cream, cornstarch, lemon zest, salt, pepper, and Parmesan.

Microwave the mixture for 30 seconds on high, then remove it from the microwave to whisk.

After whisking, microwave the mixture for another 15 seconds or so, until it's very thick.

Whisk in a few teaspoons of the lemon juice until the sauce is pourable.

Serve each pork chop with half of the asparagus spears and top with lemon cream.

NOTE: The lemon cream sauce that comes together in the microwave can easily be made on the stove—whisk together all the ingredients while cold, then heat over low heat while stirring frequently until thick.

Spicy Broccoli and Ricotta Calzones

Most days of the week we lean toward vegetarianism in my house. My husband has a deep love for calzones that stems from a brief stint during his childhood when his dad owned a pizza shop. I created a calzone that consists of just roasted veggies and gooey, creamy cheese for him.

This roasted broccoli filling isn't to be missed: the broccoli is coated in olive oil and grated Parmesan, then roasted until crisp. I also throw scallions and whole cloves of garlic onto the roasting pan. This roasted veggie filling is so good, you can also toss it with cooked farfalle pasta, ricotta, and lemon zest for a pasta dinner, too.

This recipe uses 1 pound of pizza dough to make three calzones. It's perfect—one for each person, plus an extra one to split for dessert.

2 cups fresh broccoli florets

4 scallions

2 garlic cloves, sliced in half

2 tablespoons olive oil, plus more for dough

Red pepper flakes, as much or as little as you like

¼ cup grated Parmesan

Salt

Freshly ground black pepper

Preheat the oven to 425°F.

Add the broccoli florets, whole scallions, and garlic cloves to a large baking sheet. Pour the olive oil, red pepper flakes, Parmesan, and a big pinch of salt and freshly ground pepper on top. Toss to combine. Spread the mixture evenly on the pan—don't overcrowd the pan or the veggies will steam instead of roast.

Roast the veggies for 20 minutes, until they're nicely golden brown. The ends of the scallions may be slightly burnt, but that's okay! When the veggies are done, give the scallions and garlic a rough chop and combine with the broccoli. Set aside.

¼ cup fresh ricotta (store-bought or homemade on page 41)

3 ounces fresh mozzarella, chopped into 9 pieces (or 9 bocconcini)

1 pound store-bought pizza dough

Marinara sauce, for serving

While the veggies roast, work with the pizza dough: Divide it into three even balls, and, using a floured rolling pin, roll out into three circles about 6 to 7 inches in diameter.

Line the same baking sheet used for the veggies with a piece of parchment paper. Place the dough circles on the baking sheet.

On one side of each dough circle, spread one-third of the ricotta, almost all the way to the edge.

Divide the roasted broccoli mixture on top of each dough circle and place three pieces of mozzarella into the mixture for each calzone.

Gently fold over the dough on top of the broccoli mixture. Use a fork to press each calzone closed, and then brush liberally with olive oil.

Bake for 20 to 25 minutes, until the calzones are golden brown.

Serve with small bowls of marinara for dipping.

NOTE: I don't advise frozen broccoli here, as it won't properly crisp in the oven. The best type of Parmesan for this recipe is the powdery ground Parmesan, not the shredded version.

Classic Cheese Fondue for Two

Last year we had one of the more memorable but still low-key Valentine's Day dinners that we both loved. We started out at my husband's favorite whiskey bar (yep, a whole place devoted to pre-Prohibition-era drinks), and then headed home to enjoy this classic cheese fondue. I also rounded out the meal with Chocolate Fondue for Two (page 304)

Trust me, dunking carbs in cheese sauce is a lot better than waiting for a table on the busiest restaurant night of the year!

When I make this recipe, I roast double the amount of potatoes than I think we'll eat and use them either for the Roasted Potato Bowls with Broccoli and Gribiche (page 134) or in a hash the next morning.

½ pound baby Yukon Gold
  potatoes

1 tablespoon olive oil

Salt

Freshly ground black pepper

Cornichons

Pretzels

Sliced pear

Sliced apple

Sliced French bread

4 ounces grated Gruyère

3 ounces grated Swiss cheese

3 ounces Brie, diced and rind
  removed

2 teaspoons cornstarch

½ cup dry white wine

2 teaspoons freshly squeezed
  lemon juice

½ teaspoon Dijon mustard

Preheat the oven to 400°F.

Scrub the baby potatoes and slice them in half. Spread the potatoes evenly on a large baking sheet and drizzle with the oil. Toss to coat.

Sprinkle a generous amount of salt and freshly ground black pepper over the potatoes and toss again.

Roast the potatoes until they're done, about 20 to 25 minutes. Let them cool slightly.

Place the cornichons, pretzels, sliced fruit, and bread in bowls for serving.

Next, make the fondue: Pile the grated cheeses in a bowl, add the cornstarch, and toss gently to combine.

If you have an electric fondue pot, turn it to medium. If not, use a small, heavy-bottomed pot over medium-low heat.

Add the wine, lemon juice, and Dijon mustard to the pot. Bring the mixture to a boil, then turn it down to a simmer.

Begin to slowly add the grated cheeses and diced Brie to the pot, a handful at a time, while constantly whisking.

When all the cheese has been added to the pot, turn the heat to low and whisk until everything is melted and smooth.

Serve the cheese fondue immediately with the potatoes, cornichons, pretzels, fruit, and bread. Dip and enjoy!

Soy-Roasted Mushroom and Sweet Potato Tacos

It's nearly impossible for me to grow tired of tacos, and I'm always looking for a new twist. This recipe is inspired by my dear friend Heidi Swanson, who introduced me to the idea of a freshly flame-toasted tortilla being filled with butter-roasted mushrooms in her first book, *Super Natural Cooking*. Maybe it was her enchanting photo of the tacos being enjoyed around a campfire, but I've been enamored with the idea ever since.

I roast my mushrooms and sweet potatoes in a douse of soy sauce with spices and cook them until I can see golden brown edges on each.

While the veggies roast, I make the spicy pepita cilantro pesto in the food processor and warm the tortillas. I love this pepita cilantro pesto so much because it has much less oil than regular pesto recipes, thanks to the can of fire-roasted green chiles.

FOR THE TACOS

8 ounces white button
  mushrooms
1 large sweet potato
¾ teaspoon dried oregano
¾ teaspoon smoked paprika
¼ teaspoon garlic powder
¼ teaspoon onion powder
2 tablespoons soy sauce
2 tablespoons neutral oil
4 to 6 corn tortillas

Preheat the oven to 400°F.

Clean the mushrooms by running a damp towel over each, trim off the bottom portion of the stem, and slice them in half.

Scrub the sweet potato very well, then dice it into 1-inch chunks.

In a small bowl, whisk together the spices, soy, and oil.

Spread the veggies on a large baking sheet with a 1-inch lip. Pour the spice mixture on top and toss to coat very well.

Roast the veggies for 20 minutes, or until the mushrooms and sweet potatoes have golden brown edges.

FOR THE PEPITA CILANTRO PESTO

One 4-ounce can fire-roasted
  green chiles
1 small bunch fresh cilantro
1 garlic clove
½ small yellow onion
¼ cup toasted pepitas
1 tablespoon olive oil
½ teaspoon salt
Freshly ground black pepper

Meanwhile, make the pesto: Combine all the ingredients in the bowl of a food processor and pulse until smooth.

Finally, warm the tortillas over a gas flame or wrap them in a damp paper towel and microwave them for about 15 seconds.

Scoop the filling into the tortillas (using two tortillas per taco to hold everything together), and serve with half of the pepita cilantro pesto drizzled on top.

Parmesan-Crusted Salmon with Veggies

When my garden is bursting with tomatoes and basil, all I have to do is pick up some beautiful salmon fillets at the store for dinner.

This dinner for two comes together so quickly, and I love it so much because the burst tomatoes create a sauce for everything with their juices. Don't be shy about scraping the pan to get every last drop.

Olive oil cooking spray
Two 6-ounce wild salmon
    fillets
1 small zucchini
2 pints cherry tomatoes
2 tablespoons olive oil
Salt
Freshly ground black pepper
1 small bunch fresh basil,
    chopped (or 2 teaspoons
    dried basil)
½ cup grated Parmesan

Preheat the oven to 425°F. Lightly spray a large sheet pan with cooking spray.

Gently pat the salmon dry on all sides with paper towels and place it on the sheet pan.

Cut the zucchini into sticks (see photo for reference). Surround the salmon with the tomatoes and zucchini.

Drizzle the olive oil, a big pinch of salt, and pepper on the salmon and vegetables, and toss to coat, arranging the salmon skin-side down.

Sprinkle the Parmesan and chopped (or dried) basil on everything, pressing it into the surface of the salmon.

Bake for about 10 minutes, depending on the thickness of your salmon. Test it for doneness by flaking it with a fork.

The tomatoes will be bursting and creating a sauce to spoon on everything—be sure to catch it all and spoon it over the salmon to serve.

Oven Tandoori Chicken

I have a few tricks to get my beloved tandoori chicken at home instead of driving to my favorite Indian restaurant. First, I bake it in a super hot oven and finish it under the broiler. The optional step of baking it on a wire rack over a baking sheet is totally worth it.

The list of spices called for in this recipe is long, but since this is a recipe that I make frequently, I usually have everything I need. I keep garam masala (a spice blend that most any grocery store will have) and ginger in my refrigerator just for this recipe. Use any extra garam masala when grilling meats or roasting root vegetables—the smoky, herby flavor is incredible. I serve this with homemade Naan from page 271.

¾ cup plain yogurt

1 tablespoon neutral oil

Juice of 1 lemon

1 teaspoon onion powder

1 teaspoon garlic powder

1 teaspoon fresh ginger paste

1 teaspoon garam masala

1 teaspoon ground turmeric

1 teaspoon ground cumin

1 teaspoon ground coriander

Pinch of cayenne pepper

1 teaspoon smoked paprika

1 teaspoon salt

½ teaspoon freshly ground black pepper

2 large boneless, skinless chicken breasts

Cooked basmati rice, for serving

Naan (page 271), for serving

Chopped fresh cilantro, for serving

In a small bowl, whisk together the yogurt, oil, lemon juice, all the spices, and salt and pepper. Place the chicken breasts in a shallow dish or pie plate and pour the yogurt mixture on top. Turn to coat the chicken, then cover and refrigerate 1 to 2 hours. Don't let it sit longer than 2 hours because the lemon juice will "cook" the chicken.

Preheat the oven to 400°F.

Line a sheet pan with parchment paper or foil to catch any drips.

Remove the chicken from the marinade and place it on top of a wire rack that fits on top of the sheet pan. (This is entirely optional; you can bake the chicken directly on the pan, too.)

Try to pile as much of the marinade on each side of the chicken as possible.

Bake the chicken for 15 minutes and test with a thermometer to ensure that the chicken is at least 155°F in the thickest part.

Then, turn the broiler on high and cook the chicken until it starts to blacken in a few places (about 5 minutes).

Sprinkle the chicken with cilantro and serve with hot basmati rice and naan bread.

Balsamic and Maple–Glazed Protein of Choice

I truly love this glaze on dark meat chicken cuts, but it works on pork, too. Regardless of the type of bone-in meat you use, marinate it overnight and bake at a super high temperature to ensure the sticky-sweet sauce forms.

¼ cup high-quality balsamic vinegar

¼ cup maple syrup

1 teaspoon salt

½ teaspoon freshly ground black pepper

2 sprigs fresh rosemary

1 to 2 pounds protein of choice (1 pound if boneless, 2 pounds if bone-in; 5 to 6 chicken drumsticks work great)

Whisk together all ingredients for the marinade and pour it into a large, plastic zip-top bag.

Add your protein, turn to coat, and let marinate overnight in the fridge.

When ready to cook, preheat the oven to 450°F.

Place the protein on a parchment paper–lined sheet pan and cook until it's done—use a meat thermometer to test. (For chicken drumsticks, it takes 33 to 36 minutes).

Hot Honey Lime–Glazed Protein of Choice

The first time we tasted Gwyneth Paltrow's salmon glazed with sriracha, lime, and maple syrup that took the internet by storm, we were amazed. You'll recognize similar flavors here. This hot honey-lime mixture is best used both as a quick marinade and glaze after cooking. I love it most on freshly grilled chicken, but it's great on salmon, pork, scallops, and tofu, too.

If you're marinating, cap it at no more than 2 hours so the lime juice doesn't "cook" the protein.

¼ cup honey

Zest and juice of 2 limes

½ teaspoon cayenne

1 tablespoon neutral oil

Pinch of salt

Freshly ground black pepper

1 pound protein of choice: chicken tenders, chicken breasts, pork tenderloin, scallops, tofu cubes, or anything else you like!

Whisk together all of the marinade ingredients.

Drizzle half the marinade on the protein and place it in the fridge to marinate for up to 2 hours.

If you're grilling the protein, heat the grill to high.

Place the marinated protein over the heat, flip once, and cook until done. Use a thermometer to ensure it's done, depending on the protein used.

When the meat comes off the heat, add the rest of the marinade and let it rest.

Serve immediately.

Butter-Roasted Vegetables

It feels like a good time to talk about side dishes.

My side dish game isn't strong. To be honest, it's a lot of effort most days to get a main course on the table, so I've resorted to my go-to side dishes: side salad (right outta the bag) and quick steamed broccoli. That's it. Most of the time, I make a hearty main that doesn't need a veggie side.

I dug deep to find the best way to produce vegetable side dishes. And, in the process, I discovered a simple formula: local seasonal vegetables + butter roasting = the best veggies of my life.

You don't see many vegetables roasted with butter anymore. Olive oil is doing a good thing in the oven, but it needs a little help from butter. Butter brings the flavor, crispiness, and richness. Once you've had a vegetable roasted in butter, you won't go back.

There are times (such good, good times) where I roast in all butter—usually when potatoes are involved. But most of the time, all you need is a tablespoon or two of melted butter added to the olive oil. That's it! So quick, so easy, and so much more flavor. You just might find yourself eating more vegetables, which is an excellent way to make up for all the butter.

Butter-Roasted Carrots

When I accidentally buy a new bag of carrots at the store before I finish the one from the previous week, these butter-roasted carrots become an ideal side dish.

2 pounds carrots
2 tablespoons unsalted butter
1 tablespoon neutral oil
½ teaspoon salt

Preheat the oven to 425°F.

Scrub the carrots very well, then slice them into large sticks (see photo for reference).

Spread the carrots in an even layer on a large baking sheet.

Stir together the melted butter and olive oil. Drizzle it over the carrots and toss well.

Sprinkle the salt on top and toss again.

Roast the carrots for 20 minutes, flipping after 10 minutes.

Serve hot.

Oven Fries for Special Times

When we want french fries but don't want to leave the house, I turn to the butter-roasting method for making the best oven fries. Using a sturdy baking sheet will give you the best results.

2 russet potatoes, scrubbed
    clean
2 tablespoons unsalted butter
1 tablespoon neutral oil
1 tablespoon steak seasoning
    (or 1½ teaspoons salt plus
    ½ teaspoon coarsely ground
    black pepper and 1 teaspoon
    garlic powder)

Preheat the oven to 425°F.

Scrub the potatoes very well, and then slice them into steak fry wedges (see photo for reference).

Spread the steak fries in an even layer on a large baking sheet.

Stir together the melted butter and olive oil. Drizzle it over the potatoes and toss well.

Sprinkle the steak seasoning on top and toss again.

Roast for 30 minutes, flipping after 15 minutes.

Serve hot.

Butter-Roasted Mushrooms

You would be right in thinking these would be excellent stirred into many things—warm barley (see page 138 for my Roasted Mushroom, Barley, and Brie Bowls), orzo, scrambled eggs, and even piled on top of a steak. On that note, maybe you should double this recipe.

16 ounces button mushrooms
   (2 packages)
2 tablespoons butter, melted
1 tablespoon olive oil
Handful fresh thyme (or two
   pinches dried)
Salt
Freshly ground black pepper

Preheat the oven to 400°F.

Wipe down the mushrooms quickly and place them on a parchment paper–lined baking sheet (for easy cleanup). I don't even slice the ends off first.

Stir together the melted butter and olive oil. Pour it over the mushrooms and toss.

Sprinkle the thyme, salt, and pepper on top and toss very well. Space the mushrooms out on the baking sheet—no touching!

Roast for 20 minutes, until golden brown. Wait for the caramel crust to form before removing them from the oven—it's the best part.

Melting Sweet Potatoes

These sweet potatoes are life changing. They're perfectly crisp and lightly charred on the outside, and meltingly tender on the inside.

2 pounds sweet potatoes
4 tablespoons unsalted butter, melted
½ teaspoon salt

Preheat the oven to 425°F. Have ready a large roasting pan with a 1-inch lip.

Peel and slice the sweet potatoes into 1-inch-thick slices and scatter them on the roasting pan.

Drizzle the butter on top of the sweet potatoes. Sprinkle on the salt, toss to coat, then redistribute on the pan in a single layer.

Roast for 20 minutes. Flip the potatoes with tongs and roast for another 20 minutes.

The potatoes are done when they're golden brown and crisp, and the insides are light and fluffy.

Smoked Paprika Roasted Brussels Sprouts

The combination of spoked paprika and lemon juice will brighten the flavors of almost any sturdy vegetable.

2 pounds Brussels sprouts
2 tablespoons unsalted butter, melted
1 tablespoon olive oil
½ teaspoon salt
1 tablespoon smoked paprika
Juice of 1 lemon

Preheat the oven to 425°F.

Scrub the Brussels sprouts very well, then slice off the very end of the sprout and remove any outer leaves that don't look great. Slice each sprout in half and spread the sprouts in an even layer on a large baking sheet.

Stir together the melted butter and olive oil. Drizzle it over the sprouts and toss well. Sprinkle with salt and smoked paprika and toss.

Roast the sprouts for 20 minutes, flipping after 10 minutes.

Toss with the lemon juice and serve.

CHAPTER 6.
BREAD MAKES IT
A MEAL

"Delicious Things Pinned Together with Two Slices of Bread and Other Carb-Rich Recipes" was my alternate title for this chapter. If you love sandwiches, both warm and cold, plus anything that comes off a waffle iron or grill, then this chapter is for you. If your household loves breakfast for dinner, don't miss my Cheddar Scallion Waffles. And the flavor combination of cilantro, salami, fresh corn, and creamy cheese is mind-blowing, and you'll be looking for ways to eat it beyond a grilled Pita Pizza. I also attempted to use up of the last of the baguette, since they're frequently over two feet long. Instead of requiring each member of the house to eat a foot of bread before it goes stale, I make Classic Panzanella and Pizza Baguettes that put to good use your day-old bread.

Chicken and Giardenera Subs with Marinara

Last summer, while living briefly in the Midwest, I fell in love with hot sandwiches. Specifically, I fell in love with a spicy chicken sub. There was something about the combo of a split roll, rubbed with garlic and butter, topped with grilled chicken, marinara sauce, spicy pickled veggies, and cheese that woke me up in the middle of the night with cravings.

   If you like spicy food, try subbing pepperoncini peppers for half of the giardiniera mix.

4 chicken tenders

1 tablespoon steak seasoning blend

2 teaspoons neutral oil

1 tablespoon unsalted butter

1 tablespoon olive oil

2 hoagie rolls, split

1 garlic clove, minced

½ cup jarred marinara sauce

2 slices mozzarella

½ cup giardiniera (jarred pickled vegetables)

Pepperoncini peppers, for heat (optional)

First, make the chicken for the sandwich: Toss the chicken tenders in the steak seasoning blend.

Heat the oil in an 8-inch nonstick skillet until shimmering.

Cook the chicken in the skillet until done, about 4 minutes on each side.

Remove the chicken from the skillet and slice it into pieces. Set it aside.

Preheat the broiler in the oven to low.

First, make the rolls: Melt the butter into the olive oil and stir in the minced garlic.

Brush this mixture all over the split hoagie rolls.

Toast the rolls until they're just beginning to turn light brown; don't take them too far at this point.

Remove the rolls from the oven and spread the marinara sauce evenly on the inside. Top with the sliced chicken, followed by the mozzarella.

Pile on the giardiniera (and pepperoncinis, if using), and try to squeeze the rolls closed as best as you can.

Return the sandwiches to the broiler and cook until the cheese melts and the bread is toasted, about 4 minutes.

Best-Ever Veggie Sandwiches

My veggie sandwich is not what you would expect—the flavors are decidedly Southwestern, with Mexico in the mix, too. A version of this sandwich at a little cafe in Dallas is what inspired me to keep pickled carrots in my fridge nearly year-round.

I frequently use *bolillos* as sandwich rolls, but I understand these to only be available in Texas and the Southwestern states through California. *Bolillos* are a bread roll with a slight point at each end. They're traditionally from Mexico, but I've come across them in Costa Rica a time or two. It's like a softer, fluffier baguette because, while the crust is flaky and crisp like a French baguette, the insides are softer.

But, really, use your favorite sandwich roll here—the flavors of smoky black beans, avocado, pickled carrots, and feta will be great, no matter the bread vehicle.

When I slice my *bolillos* in half, I like to remove a bit of the insides of the bread to make room for the mashed black beans.

2 teaspoons neutral oil

½ yellow onion, diced

1 garlic clove, minced

½ teaspoon smoked paprika

½ teaspoon ground cumin

1 cup cooked black beans (about half a can)

2 *bolillos* (or other sandwich sub rolls)

Pickled carrots (page 116)

¼ cup crumbled feta

1 avocado, sliced in half and pit removed

Cilantro sprouts

In a small skillet, heat the oil over medium heat and add the diced onion. Cook until it's translucent and starting to caramelize around the edges. Add the garlic, smoked paprika, and cumin and sauté for 30 seconds.

Add the beans to the skillet and stir to heat them through.

Turn off the heat and use a potato masher to mash the beans into a chunky spread. Let it cool.

Slice each *bolillo* in half and remove a bit of the bread to make room for the filling.

Generously spread the black bean mash on each roll and top with pickled carrots, feta, avocado slices, and cilantro sprouts.

Slice in half and serve with *cerveza*.

Cheddar Scallion Waffles

We're big "breakfast for dinner" fans in my house, but for me the waffles have to be savory! I serve these waffles with fried eggs and thick slices of pepper-crusted bacon.

1 cup all-purpose flour

¼ teaspoon baking soda

½ teaspoon baking powder

¾ teaspoon salt

1 tablespoon sugar

2 large eggs

1 cup buttermilk

2 tablespoons unsalted butter, melted

3 ounces (1 cup) shredded extra sharp Cheddar

3 scallions, sliced

Preheat your waffle iron to its highest setting.

Whisk together the flour, baking soda, baking powder, salt, and sugar in a large bowl. Set it aside.

Separate the eggs and place the whites in a clean bowl. Beat the whites (either by hand or with an electric mixer) until stiff peaks form, about 3 to 4 minutes.

Combine the egg yolks, buttermilk, melted butter, Cheddar, and scallions.

Add the wet ingredients to the dry ingredients and begin to fold everything together gently, being careful not to overmix.

Finally, gently fold in the beaten egg whites.

Scoop out a heaping ½ cup of batter and place it in your waffle iron. Close the lid and cook until the waffle is golden brown on both sides.

Repeat with the remaining batter. You should get four or five waffles in total, depending on the size of your iron.

Pita Pizzas with Pepita Cilantro Pesto, Salami, and Corn

My husband turned me into a grilled pizza freak. He makes his dough on Thursday night, and then he throws it on the grill Friday night—just about the time I pour the first cocktail for us to enjoy.

When he forgets to make the dough the night before, this is the way we get pita pizza on the grill instead. I use the leftover pepita cilantro pesto from the Soy-Roasted Mushroom and Sweet Potato Tacos on page 174, a few slices of salami, an ear of fresh corn, and a sprinkling of feta. This combination of flavors is something I never grow tired of all summer long!

If you have leftover Naan (page 271), they're very welcome here instead of pitas!

2 pitas

½ cup pepita cilantro pesto (page 175)

8 thin slices salami

1 ear corn, shucked and silks removed

¼ cup feta cheese

First, preheat the grill. While the grill heats, add the corn and let it slowly roast until it's charred in several places. Remove it from the heat, slice the kernels off the cob, and set aside.

When the grill is hot, oil the grates and add the pitas. Cook the pitas on one side until they begin to toast and a few grill marks form, then flip them.

Divide the cilantro pesto between the pitas and top with the salami slices, corn kernels, and feta.

Close the grill and let the pizzas cook for about 3 minutes, until the feta starts to melt slightly. Serve immediately.

Classic Panzanella

One of the woes of a small household is bread. I've never been great at freezing leftover bread (or maybe I'm just not good at defrosting it so that it tastes fresh), and so we end up with a lot of stale bread on our counter.

In the summer months, I'm happy to find stale bread on the counter because, when combined with a tangy dressing, cherry tomatoes, cucumbers, and olives, it makes the most refreshing light dinner: panzanella!

1 tablespoon white wine
   vinegar
½ teaspoon salt
½ teaspoon freshly ground
   black pepper
2 tablespoons olive oil
½ loaf stale French bread, cut
   or torn into bite-size pieces
1 cup sliced cherry tomatoes
½ cucumber, sliced
½ cup pitted Kalamata olives
¼ red onion, thinly sliced
16 fresh basil leaves

In a small bowl, whisk the vinegar, salt, and pepper together. Slowly drizzle in the olive oil while whisking. Taste the dressing and add more salt, if needed.

In a large bowl, toss the bread, tomatoes, cucumbers, olives, and red onion. Pour the dressing on top and toss to coat.

Tear the basil leaves and add them to the bowl, stirring once more before serving.

Turkey Apple Butter Grilled Cheese

Low and slow is the name of the game when it comes to grilled cheese, especially when the grilled cheese is piled as high as this one.

The first time I made this, I used leftover roasted turkey from Thanksgiving. But the flavor combo is so good that I now make it year-round with roasted turkey from the deli. You'll love this turkey sandwich with a smear of apple butter, a tangle of caramelized onions, and grated Gruyère.

The flavors of this grilled cheese will become your new favorite sandwich! You'll keep apple butter in your fridge year-round just to make this.

3 tablespoons butter

4 slices sandwich bread

4 thick slices leftover roasted turkey (or use deli meat)

¼ cup apple butter

¼ cup Pressure Cooker Caramelized Onions (page 46)

1 cup grated Gruyère

In a large nonstick skillet or griddle, melt the butter over low heat.

Place all of the bread slices in the skillet and toast them on one side.

Meanwhile, have the turkey, apple butter, caramelized onions, and grated cheese ready.

Flip two of the slices of bread when they're golden brown and toasted on one side, and divide the turkey, cheese, and caramelized onions between each slice. Flip the other bread slices, spread the freshly toasted sides with apple butter, and place them face down on top of the other two sandwiches.

Continue to cook the sandwiches on low until the cheese melts.

Remove the sandwiches from the skillet, slice them in half, and serve with your favorite chips (I love plantain chips with mine!).

Bourbon-Glazed Turkey Burgers

I think often of my Great Aunt Rose when I grill burgers. Rose definitely didn't make a bourbon glaze for her burgers, but if she were still around I would be so proud to serve these to her!

While the burgers cook, have your partner grate the Gruyère, toast the Brioche-Style Hamburger Buns (page 260), and get the sprouts ready.

Bourbon Glaze (recipe follows)
¾ pound 85% lean ground turkey
¼ teaspoon salt
¼ teaspoon freshly ground black pepper
1 tablespoon butter, if using
1 cup grated Gruyère
2 Brioche-Style Hamburger Buns (page 260)
⅓ cup fresh sprouts or micro greens

Make the burger patties: Combine the ground turkey with 1 tablespoon of the glaze, the salt, and the pepper. Gently mix everything together, taking care not to overmix. Form the mixture into two equal patties. Use your thumb to make a slight indent in the middle of each patty to help the burgers stay flat while they cook.

Preheat your grill or grill pan to high. If you're using a grill pan, add the butter to the skillet. If you're using charcoal, push the charcoal to one side so that you have a direct and indirect heat side. Add the burgers to the indirect heat side of the grill (or your grill pan over medium-high heat) and cook on the first side until golden brown.

Flip the burgers and immediately apply some of the glaze with a brush.

Continue to cook the burgers until they're done, basting a few times with the glaze.

Remove the burgers from the heat and pile the grated Gruyère on top. Cover with foil to melt the cheese and let the burgers rest.

Meanwhile, spread some glaze on each side of the bun.

Place a burger in each bun, top with sprouts, and serve.

Bourbon Glaze

⅓ cup bourbon whiskey

¼ cup ketchup

5 tablespoons dark brown
   sugar

1 tablespoon Worcestershire
   sauce

1 tablespoon apple cider
   vinegar

¼ teaspoon salt

¼ teaspoon freshly ground
   black pepper

Juice of ½ lemon

Make the bourbon glaze: In a small saucepan, combine all the ingredients except the lemon juice.

Cook over medium-high heat while stirring frequently for about 15 minutes, until the mixture starts to thicken.

Add the lemon juice and continue to cook the glaze while stirring frequently for another 5 minutes or so.

When it's done, the mixture should be reduced by more than half of the original volume. It will be thick and syrupy.

Remove the glaze from the heat and let it cool slightly.

Pizza Baguettes

If you're used to French bread pizzas, I think Pizza Baguettes will be a slight upgrade! The long, skinny baguettes tend to be thinner, which allows them to crisp up in the oven more than regular French bread. Think of this as a quick and easy way to get the flavors of a crispy, thin-crust pizza, without having to make dough from scratch!

FOR A PEPPERONI PIZZA BAGUETTE

1 baguette, sliced lengthwise and then into 5-inch pieces

¾ cup store-bought or homemade pizza sauce (recipe follows)

½ pound fresh mozzarella, sliced

Mini pepperoni

Sliced black olives

FOR A PESTO PIZZA BAGUETTE

1 baguette, sliced lengthwise and then into 5-inch pieces

½ batch spinach pesto (page 34), or ½ cup store-bought pesto

½ pound fresh mozzarella, sliced

¼ cup toasted pine nuts

Preheat the oven to 400°F.

Place the baguette pieces on the baking sheet. Spoon the sauce (either pizza sauce or spinach pesto) on top of all of the slices.

Top with the fresh mozzarella slices. Add the remaining toppings (pepperonis and black olives or pine nuts).

Bake the pizzas until the cheese melts, about 10 minutes.

Turn the broiler to high. Keep a close eye on the pizzas! Leave them under the broiler for about 3 minutes, until the edges of the baguette crisp up and the cheese begins to brown in a few places.

Serve immediately.

Quick and Easy Pizza Sauce

My favorite sauce for pizza is dead simple: all it takes is a food processor—no cooking required. While it might seem a bit weird that this sauce is essentially raw, I promise you that the bright, fresh flavor of pure tomatoes is what makes a great pizza sauce.

Just say no to the canned pizza sauce loaded with sugar and stale spices!

Half a 28-ounce can whole San Marzano tomatoes
¾ teaspoon salt
Olive oil, for pizza day!

In a food processor bowl, add the tomatoes and the salt.

Puree until mostly smooth.

The pizza sauce is ready to use as is, but I recommend brushing a bit of olive oil on the dough before spreading the sauce.

Spoon leftover pizza sauce into lightly sprayed muffin cups and freeze. Once frozen, pop out the cups and place them in a freezer-safe bag. Store for a few months for future pizzas!

Thai Peanut Roast Beef Wraps

You're looking at my desperate attempt to avoid airplane food combined with a need to use up the last of the food in the fridge before we headed away on vacation last summer. I spied my jar of red curry paste leftover from dinner earlier in the week and the last of the roast beef lunch meat in the drawer.

The flavor combo of the wrap surprised me so much that I had to make it again and again just to make sure the altitude wasn't heightening the deliciousness. Thankfully, this wrap is equally delicious on land or in the air. The flavors are unexpected and refreshing at lunchtime.

I use either shredded raw carrot or any leftover pickled carrots from making the Chicken Lettuce Cups (page 69) or Best-Ever Veggie Sandwiches (page 195). Both are great!

1 tablespoon soy sauce

2 tablespoons peanut butter

1 tablespoon red curry paste

1 teaspoon coconut sugar

2 teaspoons rice wine vinegar

2 large spinach tortillas

6 slices deli roast beef

2 Napa cabbage leaves, thinly sliced

1 carrot, grated

Cilantro sprigs, to taste

First, whisk together all of the dressing ingredients in a small bowl. Taste and adjust the seasonings, if needed. Sometimes it needs more sugar to sing or an extra splash of vinegar for a kick.

Next, lay each tortilla flat on a work surface and divide the dressing between them.

On the lower third of each tortilla, arrange half of the roast beef slices, and then pile the cabbage, carrot, and cilantro sprigs in a line on top. Roll up the tortilla by folding in the sides first and then rolling it closed. Repeat with the other tortilla.

Wrap tightly in plastic wrap and refrigerate until you're ready to eat.

CHAPTER 7.
COOK ONCE, EAT TWICE

The idea behind Cook Once, Eat Twice is to make a big batch of something and use it in several meals throughout the week. Just because we're a small household doesn't mean we shouldn't roast a whole chicken and enjoy every last bit of it. And, we shouldn't miss out on a great deal for a bulk bag of produce because we're only cooking for two. If you're new to cooking for two, this is a good place to start. At the beginning of the week, you'll prepare a large batch of a whole roasted chicken, a big pot of mashed potatoes, a batch of creamy cheese sauce, a pot of beans, or trays of roasted veggies, and work them into several dinners for two the rest of the week.

TAKE ONE
ROASTED CHICKEN . . .

Spatchcock Chicken

I am forever a fan of a good roasted whole chicken, but it can be intimidating to know when it's done cooking. If you overcook it, it will be dry; if you undercook it, well, you know how that goes.

I discovered the method of "spatchcocking" a chicken in a food magazine a few years ago and couldn't believe the results. The chicken cooks in half the time (thanks to cutting out the backbone and pressing it flat), and you get more crispy skin (thanks to the increased surface area). It's so incredible that I refuse to make a whole chicken any other way.

I'm including my method for cooking a whole spatchcock chicken in just 45 minutes, plus my favorite recipes for using up leftover chicken.

One 4- to 5-pound whole
   chicken, giblets removed
2 tablespoons unsalted butter,
   melted
1 tablespoon olive oil
Plenty of salt
Plenty of freshly ground black
   pepper

First, preheat the oven to 425°F and line a large baking sheet with a 1-inch lip with parchment paper.

Now, we spatchcock the chicken: Use kitchen shears to remove the backbone of the chicken. Begin at one end, about 1 inch over from the spine, and snip all the way to the other end. Repeat on the other side. You're cutting along both sides of the spine, and when you're done it will come out. (Personally, I save the chicken backbones to make stock in my Instant Pot, but it's up to you. I even accumulate a few backbones in a freezer bag to make a really rich stock if I don't have time to make the stock that day.)

Next, place the chicken on the baking sheet, breast side up. Using clean hands, press down firmly on the chicken to make it lie flat. You will, um, hear some bones cracking—it's fine. You want the chicken to lie flat with the legs outside. See the photos for reference.

(continued)

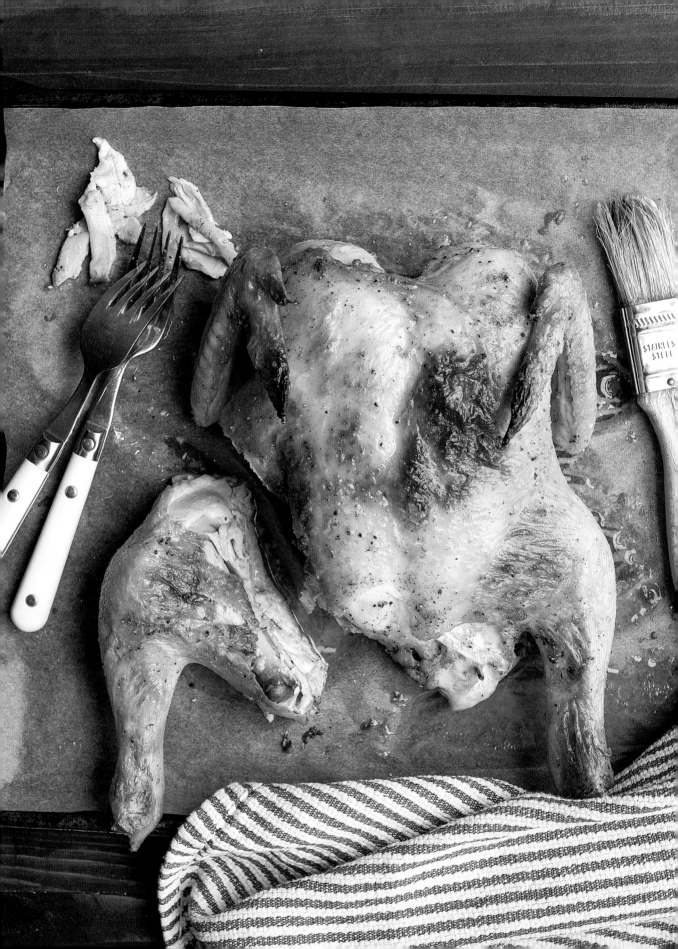

Next, combine the melted butter and olive oil, and brush it all over the entire surface of the chicken.

Sprinkle the chicken with plenty of salt and pepper on both sides.

Slide the chicken into the oven on the center rack and set a timer for 40 minutes.

After 40 minutes, use a meat thermometer to check the temperature in the thickest part of the thigh. It should register 155°F because it will continue to rise to 165°F when you remove it from the oven.

If the temperature registers at least 155°F, remove it from the oven. If not, slide it back into the oven for 5 minutes and test again.

Let the chicken cool before carving it into pieces.

Place the leftover chicken in storage containers to use later in the week for other recipes.

Creamy Chicken Enchiladas

For this recipe, you need 2 cups of "meat"—you can use all chicken or half chicken, half beans, the way I frequently do.

1 cup cooked shredded chicken

1 cup leftover beans (see page 241)

One 4-ounce can mild diced green chiles

8 ounces sour cream

1 cup jarred tomatillo salsa (it's green!)

2 cups shredded pepper Jack

4 flour tortillas

Pico de gallo, for serving

Preheat the oven to 350°F.

In a large bowl, combine the chicken, beans, and green chiles. Stir to coat.

Next, whisk together the sour cream and tomatillo salsa. Set it aside.

Pour about ¼ cup of the sour cream mixture into an 8-inch square glass or ceramic baking dish and spread it to coat the bottom of the dish.

Taking one tortilla at a time, scoop one-quarter of the chicken mixture into the lower third of the tortilla and top with a handful of shredded cheese. Roll up the tortilla tightly. Place the enchilada seam-side down in the pan. Repeat with the remaining three tortillas.

Pour the remaining sour cream mixture on top of the enchiladas in the pan and top with the remaining shredded cheese.

Bake for 20 minutes, until the cheese is melting and bubbling.

Serve with pico de gallo.

Barbecue Chicken Cornbread Casserole

Tangy barbecue sauce coats the chicken and bakes with a soft and cheesy cornbread crust. You're looking at your new favorite casserole!

1 cup cooked dark meat chicken (about 1 thigh and 1 drumstick), shredded

2 teaspoons neutral oil

1 small onion, diced

½ red bell pepper, diced

Heaping ½ cup your favorite barbecue sauce

½ cup frozen corn

One 10-ounce can tomatoes with green chiles (such as Ro-Tel)

½ cup grated sharp Cheddar

Batter from Jalapeño Cornbread Muffins (page 267)

Preheat the oven to 350°F. Have ready a small casserole dish.

In an 8-inch skillet, heat the oil over medium heat. Add the diced onion and bell pepper. Cook until softened, about 5 minutes.

Add the corn, barbecue sauce, canned tomatoes, and chiles, and heat through until bubbling.

Stir the chicken into the skillet and turn off the heat.

Pour the contents of the skillet into the small casserole dish. Set aside.

Make the cornbread muffin batter, without the jalapeños, from page 267.

Pour the cornbread muffin batter on top of the chicken mixture in the casserole dish, top with the shredded cheese, and bake for 30 minutes, until bubbling.

Southwestern Chicken Cobb Salad

I can't decide which way I prefer to serve this salad: it's so pretty when layered on a large serving platter, but honestly, it's usually just the two of us eating it on the couch in two big bowls. There's no need for fancy presentation if we're just catching up on our favorite TV shows!

FOR THE SALAD

½ bag romaine salad mix

1 cooked chicken breast, sliced or shredded

½ cup frozen corn, defrosted

1 cup black beans, rinsed

4 slices bacon, cooked

2 eggs, hard-boiled

1 cup store-bought pico de gallo

1 ripe avocado, sliced

FOR THE DRESSING

¼ cup mayonnaise

½ cup sour cream

1 tablespoon Dijon mustard

1 tablespoon honey

½ teaspoon garlic powder

½ teaspoon oregano

¼ teaspoon onion powder

½ teaspoon smoked paprika

Salt

Freshly ground black pepper

Scatter the salad mix on a large platter.

Arrange all of the other ingredients in a row, as shown in the photo (or just toss everything into a bowl and mix as you go).

Whisk together all of the dressing ingredients.

Pour the dressing on the salad, and stir to combine.

Engagement Chicken Pasta

The chicken in this recipe is based on Ina Garten's recipe for Engagement Chicken. She claims the chicken is so good that it elicits marriage proposals. While that sounds great, I'm a girl that needs some creamy pasta in order to say "yes."

A few caveats with this recipe: the cream cheese must be room temperature in order to fully incorporate and form a sauce with the hot pasta. And to that, I'll add that leftovers of this pasta aren't great because the cream cheese solidifies. So, make this and enjoy it that night. All marriage proposals can wait until after your carb-induced coma.

6 ounces spaghetti

4 tablespoons unsalted butter

10 sprigs fresh thyme

10 ounces sliced mushrooms

½ cup dry white wine

4 ounces cream cheese, softened

1 cooked chicken breast, thinly sliced

Freshly ground black pepper

Salt

2 teaspoons olive oil

Bring a large pot of salted water to a boil and cook the spaghetti according to the package directions.

Meanwhile, in a large nonstick skillet, melt the butter and thyme over medium heat.

Add the sliced mushrooms to the skillet and stir to coat them in butter. Leave them to cook for a few minutes undisturbed so that a nice crust forms. Stir and repeat until the mushrooms are golden brown. It will take about 15 minutes.

Turn the heat down to low and add the wine to the pan.

Allow the wine to cook down slightly while scraping the bottom of the pan with a wooden spoon to get all of the brown bits into the win e.

Dice the cream cheese and place it in a large bowl.

Remove the thyme sprigs from the pan and discard, then pour the contents of the pan over the cream cheese and stir until it melts. There might be a few small unmelted pieces, but the hot pasta will dissolve them.

When the pasta is done, drain it and immediately pour it over the cream cheese mixture. Toss the pasta to melt and evenly distribute the cream cheese sauce.

Divide the mixture between two bowls and serve with sliced chicken on top of each.

TAKE ONE BIG BATCH OF MASHED POTATOES . . .

Really Good Mashed Potatoes

Always tempted by a good deal, I can't help myself in the produce department. When it's nearly the same price to buy 5 pounds of potatoes versus three individual potatoes, it's time to go for the big bag.

Make the mashed potatoes early in the week and serve them with the Spatchcock Chicken (page 215) or Beef Bourguignon (page 100). Then, keep the leftovers tightly covered in the fridge for up to 5 days while you work them into Loaded Potato Soup (page 228) and Samosa Potato Patties (page 231).

5 pounds russet potatoes

1 tablespoon salt

1 cup milk

1 cup chicken broth

5 tablespoons butter

Freshly ground black pepper, to taste

Have ready a large bowl filled with cold water. Peel and coarsely chop the potatoes, placing the cubes into the cold water as you go. (The water keeps the potatoes from browning while you work your way through the entire bag.)

Once the potatoes are chopped, drain the water and add them to a large stockpot. Cover with water until it comes up about 1 inch above the potatoes. Add the salt to the water, then turn the heat to high. Bring the mixture to a gentle boil and cook until the potatoes are done. (Prick the potatoes with a knife in the pot, and if they easily slide off the knife, they're done.)

Drain the potatoes and add them back to the stockpot they were cooked in. Add the milk, chicken broth, and butter, then mash until they're smooth.

Taste the mixture, add black pepper to taste and additional salt, if needed.

Loaded Potato Soup

This is one of my mom's go-to dinners on a cold night. I can't handle a huge pot of leftovers, so I scaled it down to use leftover mashed potatoes and the last few slices of bacon from the package. So comforting!

2 slices bacon

½ yellow onion, diced

½ teaspoon salt

2 garlic cloves, minced

3 cups Really Good Mashed
  Potatoes (page 227)

2 cups chicken broth

2 tablespoons unsalted butter

Freshly ground black pepper,
  to taste

½ cup shredded sharp Cheddar

1 scallion, sliced

In a small stockpot, add the bacon strips. Turn the heat to medium and cook the bacon until it releases its fat and is almost (but not quite) crispy, about 4 minutes on each side. Remove the bacon strips from the pan and let them cool on a paper towel–lined plate.

In the pot with the rendered bacon drippings, add the chopped onion and salt. Cook the onion until it starts to turn translucent and softens. Add the garlic and cook for another 30 seconds.

Stir in the mashed potatoes, chicken broth, and butter. Heat the mixture through. Taste and add more salt and black pepper, if desired.

Divide the soup between two bowls and top with the cheese, bacon slices, and sliced scallions.

Samosa Potato Patties

The flavors of a vegetarian samosa are something I'm always craving. My favorite samosas are stuffed with potatoes, peas, and plenty of spices. If you've never had a samosa, it's a type of Indian dumpling stuffed with potatoes and spices. It's essentially a carb wrapped in a carb, which always means comfort to me.

I've replicated the flavors of a samosa in a much easier way—leftover potatoes doctored up with spices and peas and fried into a crisp, craveable patty. It reminds me of the days when I first met my husband, and our go-to lunch date was at the Indian restaurant on the campus of University of California, Davis.

¼ yellow onion

1 teaspoon turmeric powder

1 teaspoon ground cumin

1 teaspoon garam masala

Dash of cayenne (optional)

Juice of ½ lemon, plus lemon slices for garnish

½ teaspoon salt

Freshly ground black pepper

2 cups Really Good Mashed Potatoes (page 227)

2 large eggs, beaten

½ cup peas (defrosted, if frozen)

½ cup whole wheat panko bread crumbs (plus more, if needed)

¼ cup olive oil

Grate the onion on the large holes of a box grater. Add the grated onion to a large bowl and stir in all the other ingredients, except the panko bread crumbs and the olive oil.

Once the mixture is homogenous, add ½ cup of bread crumbs and stir to combine. The mixture should be thick and have the texture of cold, leftover mashed potatoes. Let it sit for 5 minutes and add additional bread crumbs a few tablespoons at a time, if necessary, to achieve the appropriate texture.

Using a ½-cup measure, scoop out the potato mixture and flatten it into a 4- to 5-inch patty using your hands.

Heat the olive oil in a nonstick skillet until it's very hot. Fry the patties until they're golden brown, about 3 minutes on each side.

Serve with extra lemon slices.

TAKE ONE BIG BATCH OF CHEESE SAUCE . . .

Master Cheese Sauce

We're making a big pot of béchamel sauce (or cheese sauce—same thing) and using it to make three cozy dinners for two. This is the first thing I make when I feel like fall has arrived, which happens to usually be around my birthday! Creamy, cheesy dinners for my birthday week (you celebrate all week, don't you?) plus apple cobbler for dessert make me so happy to turn a year older . . . and so happy that it's finally fall!

A few recipe notes:

- I use 2% milk because that's what we usually have in the fridge. Whole milk is even better!
- I once made this recipe with mild Cheddar and I felt like it was missing something. Always reach for sharp or extra sharp for maximum flavor!
- If the quantity of salt gives you pause, consider that we will be dividing this batch of cheese sauce up over three recipes, and no additional salt will be added to those recipes. Take the plunge!

1 stick unsalted butter

½ cup all-purpose flour

4 cups milk (2% or whole)

1 tablespoon kosher salt (yes, really)

½ teaspoon onion powder

4 cups grated sharp or extra sharp Cheddar

Freshly ground black pepper

In a 2-quart saucepan, melt the butter over low heat. When the butter is fully melted, stir in the flour and cook while constantly stirring for about 1 minute. It will start to smell a little nutty—this lets you know the flour is cooked.

Stir in the milk slowly, followed by the salt and onion powder.

Bring the mixture to a gentle simmer while stirring occasionally, about 8 to 10 minutes.

Stir in the grated cheese a handful at a time, stirring constantly until it's smooth and creamy.

Taste, adjust with salt and pepper for seasoning, and turn off heat.

Use the amount of cheese sauce you need right away for any of the recipes below. Store the leftover sauce covered tightly in the fridge for up to 5 days. Yes, it will congeal, but heat (and maybe a splash of milk) will smooth it out.

Broccoli Cheese Soup

Arguably one of the best ways to eat your broccoli! This soup comes together in 15 minutes flat, thanks to the cheese sauce prepared ahead of time.

1 tablespoon unsalted butter
½ yellow onion, finely diced
⅓ cup shredded carrot
1 medium stalk broccoli, chopped
1½ cups chicken broth
¼ teaspoon dry mustard powder
2 cups Master Cheese Sauce (page 233)
Freshly ground black pepper
Grated Cheddar, for serving (optional)

In a 2-quart saucepan, melt the butter over medium heat. Add the diced onion and cook while stirring occasionally for about 5 minutes. The onions will soften and become translucent—if the edges start browning, stir the pot more frequently and turn down the heat.

Add the carrot, broccoli, chicken broth, and mustard powder. Bring the mixture to a simmer to cook the broccoli.

Stir in the cheese sauce and cook until it's melted and smooth.

Give the soup a taste and stir in salt (between the broth and cheese sauce, mine usually doesn't need any) and black pepper to taste.

If you like, you can ladle this into bowls and serve with grated Cheddar on top.

Totchos

Have you heard of totchos? They're nachos made with tater tots! I wish I hadn't heard of totchos. They're my favorite way to be bad. My favorite carb topped with cheese topped with bacon. And sour cream. Oh, boy.

My husband and I accidentally discovered totchos at a baseball game. We were all set to order nachos, but the person in front of us ordered totchos. Intrigued, we said, "We'll have the same," and life has never been the same.

If you don't wish to delve into the naughty world of using tater tots as nachos, feel free to use tortilla chips!

Half a 1-pound package of
  frozen tater tots
1 cup Master Cheese Sauce
  (page 233)
½ pound ground beef, ground
  turkey, or bacon
¼ cup sour cream, for serving
¼ cup salsa, for serving
Scallions, for serving

Preheat the oven to 400 to 450°F (whatever temperature your bag of tater tots recommends).

When the oven is hot, spread the tater tots in a single layer on a baking sheet and slide the sheet into the oven. Bake for the time recommended on the package.

Meanwhile, cook the ground meat or bacon in a skillet until no longer pink. Break it up with a wooden spoon while it cooks. Drain the mixture and set aside.

When the tater tots are done, remove from the oven but keep the oven on.

Spread the cheese sauce on top of the tater tots, followed by the cooked meat. Slide the sheet pan back into the oven and cook until the cheese starts to bubble in a few places.

Serve with dollops of sour cream, salsa, and scallions on top.

Green Chile Mac & Cheese

If green chiles are on the menu at a restaurant, 10 times out of 10 I'm ordering them. I lived through a nightmare once: my husband and I ordered separate burgers at a restaurant (we normally split meals out), and he ordered the world's most perfect green chile cheeseburger with crushed tortilla chips on top. I've never had greater order envy in my life! This was at least three years ago, and I'm still sitting here, mulling on it. Whenever the memory surfaces, I make this Green Chile Mac & Cheese.

A little splash of Cholula on top is welcome, too!

1½ cups dry macaroni

1½ cups Master Cheese Sauce (page 233)

½ teaspoon smoked paprika

One 4-ounce can roasted green chiles, chopped (see Note)

Bring a large pot of salted water to a boil and cook the macaroni according to the package directions.

Meanwhile, warm up the cheese sauce either in the microwave or in a small saucepan. Stir in the smoked paprika and green chiles.

When the macaroni is done cooking, toss it with the cheese sauce and serve.

NOTE: Canned roasted chiles come in mild or spicy; use whichever you prefer.

TAKE ONE BIG BATCH OF BEANS . . .

A Good Pot of Beans

I'm such a fan of beans that I will always advocate for making them from scratch. When cooking for two, you have a few options. Since most bags of dried beans are 1 pound, you can either cook only half of the bag at a time, or cook it all and freeze some.

If you're going to cook the whole dang bag (which is what I almost always opt for), plan to use them in two different recipes that week. You're still going to have about 2 cups left over, but, scooped into freezer-safe bags or jars, they keep for a few months. Frozen, defrosted cooked beans are best suited to soups or refried uses, as the ice crystals in the freezer can cause the skins to split when reheated.

The most important thing when making a pot of beans is to find high-quality beans. If you're buying them from a store, make sure it has a high turnover rate (usually health food store bulk bins get refilled several times a week). My favorite place to buy beans is online from a dude who loves beans more than me (his name is Steve Sando and his company is Rancho Gordo). I've bought many of his beans over the years, but I always come back to the cranberry bean. Also called the borlotti bean, it's quite common in grocery stores, too—especially in the Italian section. I bought my last bag at a *salumeria* (an Italian specialty foods store). They were imported from Italy, plump, shiny, and begging me to cook them.

Do I sound bean obsessed? I totally am. One of my favorite dinners growing up was when my mom put a bag of navy beans in the crockpot with a huge chopped onion and gobs of black pepper. It was simple, and I still turn to that meal when I need some comfort. It's hard to believe so few ingredients can taste so good.

So, first, let's make a pot of beans! The method here is very precise; read the recipe in its entirety before proceeding. I always advocate for adding salt after beans have cooked. If you don't have fresh herbs (totally fine!), use four bay leaves.

1 pound cranberry beans,
  picked over and rinsed
½ medium yellow onion,
  chopped in half
2 hearty sprigs fresh rosemary
½ teaspoon freshly ground
  black pepper
1 tablespoon salt

Rinse the beans very well, then place them in a deep bowl. Completely submerge them in water, giving them at least an extra 3 inches of water on top to ensure they have enough room to expand.

Soak the beans at room temperature for at least 12 hours and up to 24.

When you're ready to cook the beans, drain and rinse them one last time.

Place the beans in a large stockpot with the onion, rosemary, and black pepper. Add enough water to the pot to cover the beans, plus about 2 inches.

Turn the heat to medium-high and bring the beans to a brief boil. Lower the heat to a gentle simmer and continue to cook them for about 45 to 60 minutes.

Taste at least four beans from the pot to ensure they are done. They should be tender all the way through and the skins should be soft. If not, continue to simmer and check them again every 10 minutes.

Turn the heat off, add the salt, and stir to dissolve. Let the beans sit and come to room temperature on the stove.

Store the beans in their cooking liquid in the fridge until you need them (I always steal a bowl of them plain, right away).

Or, You Make Beans in the Pressure Cooker

When I make beans in the Instant Pot, it's usually because I want to use them several ways throughout the week, so I leave out the onion. This way, my beans are more "plain" and can take on the flavors of the specific dish.

1 pound beans, soaked
  overnight
1 tablespoon salt

Drain the beans from their soaking liquid and give them a quick rinse in a strainer.

Place the beans in the bottom of the Instant Pot and cover the beans with enough water to come up to an inch above the beans.

Place the lid on the Instant Pot, turn the valve to "Seal," and cook on high pressure for 8 minutes.

When the timer goes off, let the beans do a natural pressure release.

When the seal releases (make sure the metal valve has dropped), remove the lid, and stir in the salt.

Let the beans sit for about 5 minutes, then taste them for seasoning.

Store the beans in their liquid in the fridge, or drain and freeze for later use.

Best-Ever Bean Burgers

I've had a lot of bean burgers and veggie burgers in my day (no judgments, please) and found most of them to be overly soft. It wasn't until I started including corn-meal in the mix that my bean burgers started staying together and having a pleasing texture with a crisp outside.

The bean patties must be refrigerated for at least 2 hours (and up to 24 hours) before you attempt to cook them, so plan accordingly.

¼ cup olive oil, divided

4 button mushrooms, finely diced

4 sprigs fresh thyme

½ small onion, diced

1 garlic clove, minced

1 cup cooked beans, drained

1 tablespoon mayonnaise, plus more for serving

2 teaspoons fresh lemon juice

¼ cup yellow cornmeal, plus extra for dredging

¾ teaspoon salt

¼ teaspoon freshly ground black pepper

2 Brioche-Style Hamburger Buns (page 260)

Lettuce

Sliced tomatoes

In a small skillet, heat 2 tablespoons of the olive oil over medium heat. Sauté the mushrooms until they soften, release their juices, and then begin to turn golden brown, about 5 minutes.

Once the mushrooms have browned, stir in the thyme sprigs and onion and cook until they're softened, another 5 minutes.

Finally, stir in the garlic and cook until it's fragrant, about 30 seconds.

Pour the mushroom mixture into a food processor, removing the thyme sprigs (most of the leaves should have fallen off in the pan; don't put the woody stems in the food processor!). Puree until smooth and set aside.

Add the drained beans to the food processor and puree until smooth.

Combine the mushroom mixture and pureed beans in a large bowl. Stir in all remaining burger ingredients.

Divide the mixture in half to form two patties. Spread some extra cornmeal on a plate and place both patties on top. Gently flip to coat both patties in the cornmeal, then refrigerate for at least 2 hours or up to 24 hours.

When you're ready to cook the patties, remove them from the fridge and flip them again in the cornmeal, trying to get as much cornmeal as possible to adhere to the patties.

Heat the remaining olive oil in a small nonstick skillet over medium-low heat. Add the patties to the pan and cook over low heat. Do not flip the patties until a golden brown crust forms on the first side. Medium-low heat is perfect for creating a firm crust without burning them.

Flip the patties and cook them on the remaining side. Let them rest for a few minutes before piling them on top of burger buns with lettuce, tomato, and more mayonnaise (or whatever you like on your burger).

My Famous Refried Beans

I've tried a few refried beans recipes that have the words "healthy," "light," or "lower in fat" in the recipe title. What that really means is that your beans will resemble a paste not unlike wallpaper glue. No, no, no. Just no.

Refried beans really need some fat to become smooth and silky (which is everything they're meant to be), but my pantry never has lard in it. A few slices of bacon step up to the plate, and everything is as it should be.

During my brief stint as a private chef, I made many batches of these beans as a side dish for any Mexican-inspired meal. They always received so much praise.

3 to 4 bacon slices (choose
    your own adventure here—
    I use 3 slices, but 4 is
    amazing)
2 cups cooked beans, drained
Freshly ground black pepper
Salt (optional)

Add the bacon slices to the bottom of a heavy pan (I love my mini Dutch oven for this). Turn the heat to medium and cook the bacon until it releases its fat and starts to crisp around the edges.

Remove the bacon from the pan with a slotted spoon, leaving the fat in the pan.

Add the beans to the pan and, using a potato masher, mash the beans into a creamy mixture.

Add pepper to taste. Add salt if you think it needs it.

You can serve these as is or with the bacon crumbled on top.

Simple Rosemary Bean Soup

If you didn't read my "beans from scratch" manifesto on page 241, I don't blame you one bit. There are a lot of great canned beans at the store. The only caveat is that all beans in cans need a very thorough rinse before using.

This recipe will work with one can of white beans (rinsed), or with a scant 2 cups of homemade beans. I will say, though, that canned beans could use a little help in the flavor department, and one slice of chopped bacon cooked in the skillet with the onions can do wonders as a flavor boost.

This recipe only uses half an onion, as does the recipe for cooking the beans from scratch. Similarly, this recipe uses a sprig of rosemary, also leftover from cooking the beans from scratch.

1 tablespoon olive oil, plus extra for serving
½ medium yellow onion, finely diced
1 garlic clove, minced
2 cups cooked beans (or 1 can white beans, rinsed)
1 cup chicken broth
1 sprig fresh rosemary
Freshly ground black pepper

In a 2-quart saucepan, add the olive oil and heat over medium heat for about 40 seconds. Add the finely diced onion and sauté until the edges start to brown and the onion is golden, about 5 minutes.

Add the minced garlic clove and cook for 1 minute.

Stir in the beans, chicken broth, rosemary, and black pepper. Bring everything to a gentle simmer and cook for about 5 minutes.

Give it a taste—I find that this soup doesn't need any salt because the beans are adequately seasoned, but add salt if it tastes flat.

Remove the rosemary sprig, divide the soup between two bowls, and serve with a drizzle of olive oil on top.

I almost always serve these with a small batch of Jalapeño Cornbread Muffins (page 267).

TAKE ONE BIG BATCH OF ROASTED VEGGIES . . .

Roasted Veggies

Roasting a giant tray of vegetables (well, two trays in this case) is sometimes the only way I can work veggies into dinners during a busy week.

I chop up a big russet potato, a big sweet potato, a couple carrots, and a bunch of mushrooms. I like to add beets if I have them, even though they sort of drive me batty because they stain the other veggies pink. But beets are healthy, so I deal with it!

These roasted veggies are great to have on hand in the fridge for rounding out any dinner, and I've even been known to toss the roasted sweet potatoes and carrots into a breakfast smoothie. Yes, really! Add some vanilla yogurt and cinnamon, and you'll have a thick smoothie reminiscent of pie.

Other delicious additions: huge chunks of cauliflower (big so they cook in the same amount of time as the starchy root vegetables), zucchini half-moons (and other squash) in the summer months, Brussels sprouts halves, bell pepper chunks, and onion slices for their sweet caramelization potential.

I like to add big sprigs of thyme and rosemary that I snipped from the garden, but a heavy hand with a jar of mixed dried Italian herbs is great!

First, I'd like to go over the proper way to roast vegetables because a few missteps will leave you with soggy, steamed vegetables:

- Use two big sheet pans with a 1-inch lip, not flat cookie sheets.
- Crowding the vegetables on the pan will cause them to steam, which significantly lowers the chances of delicious, golden brown, crusty edges. Use two pans.
- Two tablespoons of olive oil is plenty for each pan; a light coating of oil is the goal.
- Three-quarters of a teaspoon of kosher salt per tray is ideal, and as much freshly ground black pepper as you're inclined.
- Make two big trays of these herby roasted vegetables and use them throughout the week in several dinners for two.

(continued)

1 large russet potato

1 large sweet potato

2 medium beets

2 carrots

4 to 6 ounces of your favorite
mushrooms (I used shiitake
here)

4 tablespoons olive oil, divided

1½ teaspoons kosher salt,
divided

Freshly ground black pepper

Herbs: rosemary sprigs, sage
leaves, and thyme sprigs

Preheat the oven to 400°F.

Have two heavy, large baking sheets with 1-inch
rims ready.

Chop the potato and sweet potato (I leave the
skin on these) into 1- to 2-inch chunks.

Next, peel the carrots and beets. Chop into 1- to
2-inch chunks.

If the mushrooms are small, leave them whole; if
not, chop them in half.

Divide the mixture evenly between the two
baking sheets.

Drizzle 2 tablespoons of olive oil on each sheet,
followed by ¾ teaspoon of salt on each sheet.
Grind black pepper on top of each sheet and
sprinkle the herbs on top.

Using your hands, toss the mixture together to
coat everything in oil.

Spread the mixture out as much as possible.

Place the pans in the oven on the middle and
lower racks.

Roast for 30 minutes, rotating the pans after 15
minutes.

Let the veggies cool slightly before storing them
in the fridge for future meals.

Veggie Hash Under Eggs

Just put eggs on top of those veggies!

1 tablespoon olive oil, plus
    extra for drizzling
1 cup Roasted Veggies (page
    249)
2 large eggs
Salt
Freshly ground black pepper

In a nonstick skillet, heat 1 tablespoon of olive oil over medium heat. Add the roasted veggies and cook, stirring occasionally, to warm them through.

Divide the veggies between two plates and set them aside.

Next, add another splash of olive oil, then crack each egg into the skillet, one at a time.

Fry the eggs until they're done to your liking, tilting the pan and spooning the hot olive oil over the top of the eggs as they cook.

Slide a fried egg onto each plate over the hash, and serve with an extra drizzle of olive oil.

Veggie Hash Over Pasta

Now, put the roasted veggies on top of pasta!

6 ounces short pasta (such as whole wheat penne)

1 cup Roasted Veggies (if refrigerated, let come to room temperature; page 249)

¼ cup mascarpone

¼ cup Parmesan

Salt

Freshly ground black pepper

Bring a large pot of water to a boil. Salt the water and add the pasta, cooking according to the package directions.

Drain the pasta, reserving about ½ cup of the pasta water.

In a large bowl, toss the drained pasta, pasta water, veggies, mascarpone, and Parmesan.

Toss very well to melt the cheeses; taste and add more Parmesan, salt, and pepper, if desired.

Cacio e Pepe Polenta Casserole

With the last scoop or two of roasted veggies, make this polenta casserole that has the flavors of cacio e pepe baked right in, with plenty of Pecorino Romano and freshly ground black pepper.

Olive oil cooking spray

2½ cups whole milk

½ teaspoon salt

½ cup quick-cooking polenta (coarse cornmeal)

½ cup Pecorino Romano

2 tablespoons butter

Freshly ground black pepper

1½ cups Roasted Veggies (page 249)

½ cup grated mozzarella (for a gooey effect) or Parmesan

Preheat the oven to 400°F.

Spray an 8-inch square pan with cooking spray.

In a medium saucepan, add the milk, salt, 1½ cups water. Bring to a boil.

Slowly pour in the polenta while whisking the mixture.

When all of the polenta is in the pot, continue to cook over medium heat until the mixture absorbs all of the liquid and starts to thicken in the pan, usually 5 minutes or less. Stir constantly.

Remove the thickened polenta from the heat and stir in the Pecorino Romano and butter. Stir until it's melted and smooth. Add plenty of freshly ground black pepper.

Pour the mixture into the baking dish and top with the roasted veggies.

Sprinkle mozzarella or Parmesan on top and bake for 10 minutes.

Serve hot.

CHAPTER 8. SMALL-BATCH BREAD

I've hinted at it several times now, but whole loaves of bread just don't work in the small household. Even if I remember to freeze the rest of a baguette or sliced loaf, I don't always remember the bread is there or how to defrost it properly. So, I created these small-batch bread recipes. I have all the basics here: hamburger buns, dinner rolls, and a small crusty boule. I've also included focaccia for a date night cheeseboard, spicy cornbread, biscuits, and naan, too!

Focaccia

Focaccia is one of my favorite snacking breads, as in, I don't need a reason to eat this bread. It's an excellent vehicle for high-quality, local olive oil and fresh rosemary from the garden. It's equally welcome next to a bowl of pasta or on a cheese board spread.

If you have very coarse salt, it's great sprinkled on top.

Makes 8 slices

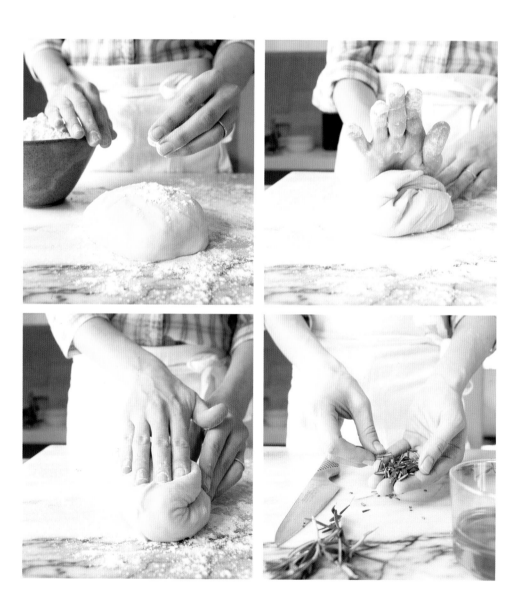

1½ teaspoons active dry yeast

1 teaspoon sugar

300 grams (about 2½ cups) all-purpose flour

1 teaspoon salt, plus extra for sprinkling on top

½ cup olive oil, divided

3 sprigs fresh rosemary

Place ¾ cup of barely warm water (105 to 110°F is ideal) in a small bowl, then stir in the yeast and sugar. Let the yeast mixture bloom for about 5 minutes. After 5 minutes, it should be foamy on the surface.

Meanwhile, add the flour, salt, and half of the olive oil (¼ cup) to a mini stand mixer fitted with the dough hook and beat briefly to combine.

Pour the yeast mixture into the flour mixture. Turn the mixer to medium and knead for 5 minutes. Stop and scrape the dough down every minute or so.

At the end of 5 minutes, the dough may be slightly sticky, but that's fine.

On a well-floured surface, knead the dough for about 30 seconds—the stickiness will completely disappear.

Place the dough in a small, greased bowl. Let the dough rise in a warm place for about an hour, or until it has doubled in size.

Pour 2 tablespoons of the remaining olive oil on a quarter sheet pan (measuring 9 by 13 inches) and spread it evenly. Add the dough to the pan and use your fingers to spread it to the corners of the pan. Try not to make too many holes, but some are okay.

Brush the final 2 tablespoons of olive oil on top of the dough and place the sheet pan in a warm place to rise until the dough doubles again, about 1 hour.

Preheat the oven to 425°F.

Sprinkle the rosemary on top of the dough and sprinkle additional salt (coarse is fun here) on top.

Bake the bread for 18 to 21 minutes, until it starts to turn a light golden brown.

Immediately after baking, flip the bread onto a cooling rack (do not let it cool in the pan). Let it cool completely before slicing and serving.

NOTE: To make this without a stand mixer, knead by hand for 10 minutes.

Brioche-Style Hamburger Buns

The best burgers are served on a brioche bun. Brioche is a rich, egg-based dough that is super soft yet holds its shape. I've created a smaller version of it here with a touch of whole wheat flour.

   This recipe gets made at least once a week in my house during the summer, but know that you can double the recipe and freeze the extra buns.

Makes 4 buns

½ cup whole milk

1 teaspoon active dry yeast

1 tablespoon sugar, plus a
   pinch extra

1 tablespoon softened butter

1 large egg, beaten, plus one
   egg yolk, beaten

1 cup all-purpose flour

½ cup whole wheat flour

¾ teaspoon salt

3 tablespoons sesame seeds
   (optional)

In a small saucepan, scald the milk (scalding is heating until small bubbles form around the edges of the pan and steam rises from the surface, but never boiling).

Remove the milk from the heat and add 1 tablespoon water. Stir and let sit until it cools to about 105°F.

Once the milk-water mixture is the right temperature, stir in the yeast and just a pinch of the sugar. Let the yeast mixture bloom, about 5 minutes. After 5 minutes, it should be foamy on the surface.

Stir the butter and the whole egg into the milk and yeast mixture (don't worry if the butter doesn't melt all the way immediately).

Add the liquid ingredients to a mini stand mixer fitted with the dough hook and beat briefly to combine.

In a small bowl, whisk together both flours with the salt and the sugar.

While the mixer is running, add the dry ingredients in two batches.

Crank the mixer to medium-high and knead for 8 to 10 minutes. The dough will be sticky.

Place the dough in a well-oiled bowl, turning it to coat with oil. Cover the bowl loosely with plastic wrap and let the dough rise in a warm place for about 2 hours, or until it has doubled in size. (Rising time is dependent on the temperature of the room; let rise until the dough is doubled.)

Punch the dough down very well and gather it into a ball.

Weigh the dough and divide into four pieces—each should weigh between 95 and 97 grams.

Roll each dough piece into a ball, then use your fingers to pinch the edges under until the seam is on the bottom. Then, cup your hand over the dough ball on the counter and make circles on the counter with the dough to roll it into a perfect ball.

Repeat with the other three pieces of dough.

Place the four dough balls on a baking sheet and cover loosely with plastic wrap. Place the sheet in a warm place to rise for 1 hour. They will be puffy when ready.

Meanwhile, preheat the oven to 375°F.

Finally, make the topping: Whisk the egg yolk with a splash of water. Brush generously on each bun, covering the entire surface, and then sprinkle with sesame seeds.

Bake for 16 to 19 minutes, until they're deeply golden brown.

Perfect Dinner Rolls

Soft, fluffy dinner rolls are coveted in my family. These dinner rolls have just the right amount of yeast and honey, and they're as soft and fluffy as cotton candy inside. I could eat an entire pan of these, so it's a good thing the recipe only makes four rolls. I bake these in a mini 6-inch cake pan (which is what I bake mini cakes in; you can find one at the hobby store), but if you lack the pan, try a muffin pan.

Makes 4 rolls

¼ cup milk
2 teaspoons honey
½ teaspoon active dry yeast
2 large egg yolks, divided
1 tablespoon melted butter
¼ teaspoon salt
1 cup all-purpose flour
Nonstick cooking spray

In a small microwave-safe bowl, add the milk and honey. Heat the mixture in the microwave for about 20 seconds until the temperature is 115°F.

Whisk the mixture to dissolve the honey into the milk. Stir in the yeast and let it bloom for about 5 minutes. After 5 minutes, it should be foamy on the surface.

Stir in one egg yolk and the melted butter.

In a separate bowl, add the flour and salt and stir them together with a fork.

Pour the wet ingredients on top of the flour mixture and stir until it starts to come together.

Knead the dough for a few minutes in the bowl. It will be sticky and pliable. Cover and let the dough rise in a warm place until it has doubled in size.

Once it has doubled, preheat the oven to 375°F.

Divide the dough into four equal pieces and roll each piece into a perfect ball. You can pinch from underneath the dough to make the top perfectly smooth, but it's not necessary.

Place the dough balls into a 6-inch round cake pan that has been lightly sprayed with cooking spray (or use a muffin pan).

Let the dough rise while the oven preheats. Ideally, the dough balls will be puffy and touching each other before they go in the oven.

Brush the dough with the remaining egg yolk.

Bake on the middle rack for 18 to 19 minutes, until they are golden brown.

Remove them from the oven and let them cool for about 5 minutes before tearing apart and serving.

Jalapeño Cornbread Muffins

I make a batch of these muffins a few times a month because I happen to think cornbread is an excellent morning food—not quite as sweet as a muffin but still just as comforting. You may absolutely leave out the jalapeños if you don't like your mornings too spicy, of course.

Makes 6 muffins

½ cup finely ground yellow cornmeal

⅓ cup all-purpose flour

1 tablespoon granulated sugar

¾ teaspoon baking powder

⅛ teaspoon baking soda

¼ teaspoon salt

1 large egg

½ cup buttermilk

1 small jalapeño, diced, plus extra for topping, if desired

2 tablespoons unsalted butter, melted

Preheat the oven to 400°F. Line a muffin tin with six liners.

In a medium bowl, whisk together the cornmeal, flour, sugar, baking powder, baking soda, and salt.

In a glass measuring cup, beat the egg into the buttermilk and stir in the diced jalapeño. Add this mixture to the dry ingredients.

Stir until combined, then stir in the melted butter.

Divide the batter between the muffin cups, top with extra diced jalapeños (if desired), and bake for 12 to 13 minutes. The muffins are done when the tops spring back when pressed on.

Serve the muffins warm with salted butter.

Cheddar Garlic Biscuits

Warm melted butter and cold buttermilk are the keys to these super flaky biscuits that taste just like the ones from a certain crustacean restaurant, if you know what I mean.

They have two kinds of cheese (grated Cheddar and Parmesan) and a heaping ½ teaspoon of garlic powder.

It's a very good thing this recipe only makes four biscuits because I could probably eat a whole tray of these!

Makes 4 biscuits

1 cup all-purpose flour
1 teaspoon baking powder
¼ teaspoon baking soda
¼ teaspoon salt
½ teaspoon garlic powder
¼ cup ground Parmesan
5 tablespoons melted butter, divided
½ cup cold buttermilk (low fat is fine)
½ cup grated extra sharp Cheddar
Fresh parsley, for serving

Preheat the oven to 475°F.

Line a small baking sheet with parchment paper or a silicone mat.

In a medium bowl, whisk together the flour, baking powder, baking soda, salt, garlic powder, and Parmesan.

In a microwave-safe bowl, melt the butter. Reserve 1 tablespoon for brushing on the biscuits later.

Add 4 tablespoons of the melted butter to the cold buttermilk and stir.

Pour the buttermilk mixture and the grated Cheddar into the dry ingredients and stir just until it comes together. Don't overmix or you'll get tough biscuits!

Press the dough flat in the bowl and score it into four equal pieces.

Scoop out each quarter of the dough onto the baking sheet. Pile the dough high on top of itself and leave it rough on the edges.

Brush the remaining tablespoon of melted butter on the biscuits.

Bake for 14 minutes, until the bottoms are golden brown and the tops are crispy.

Serve warm with fresh parsley and enjoy!

Naan

Naan is one of my favorites for so many reasons—I love that it uses up the last of the Greek yogurt in the container, and I love that it is the perfect vehicle for scooping sauces. I also love it on its own as a snack, drenched in garlicky melted butter.

This recipe makes just four naan, which is perfect for a dinner for two, plus two left over to replace the pita in Pita Pizzas with Pepita Cilantro Pesto, Salami, and Corn (page 199).

Makes 4 naan

¼ cup warm milk (110°F)
1 teaspoon sugar
½ teaspoon active dry yeast
⅓ cup Greek yogurt, at room
    temperature preferred
1⅓ cup all-purpose flour
Pinch of salt
Butter, for cooking and serving

In a small bowl, whisk together 1 tablespoon warm water (110°F), the warm milk, sugar, and yeast. Let the yeast mixture bloom, about 5 minutes. After 5 minutes, it should be foamy.

Next, stir in the yogurt, flour, and salt. Cover the dough and let it rise in a warm place for about an hour.

When you're ready to cook, heat a cast-iron skillet over high heat until it's very hot.

Punch down the dough and divide it into four equal pieces. Flour a work surface and roll the dough out into a rough oval shape.

Melt enough butter to coat the pan and gently place one piece of dough into the skillet.

In just 2 to 3 minutes, the dough will release from the pan and brown spots will start to form.

Flip and cook on the other side until brown spots form.

Repeat with the remaining dough, keeping the cooked naan bread warm by wrapping it in a towel.

To store any leftover naan, place it in an airtight container. Rewarm it gently in a skillet before serving.

No-Knead Dutch Oven Bread

When I found out that mini Dutch oven pots existed, I felt like they were made for me. My mom gave me the 3.5-quart mini, and honestly life has never been the same. I use it to make all of my small-batch soups and stews, but also this no-knead bread recipe!

You have to start this no-knead dough the night before, but you just leave it on the counter, no stirring or kneading required! When you're ready to bake the next day, preheat the oven with your pot in it, carefully remove the lid, and plop in the dough. You will be so shocked at how good the final result is!

Makes 1 mini boule

3 cups all-purpose flour
1¾ teaspoons salt
½ teaspoon active dry yeast

In a large bowl, stir together the flour, salt, and yeast. Pour 1½ cups plus 1 tablespoon warm water (about 110°F) on top, and stir just to combine.

Cover the bowl with plastic wrap (poke a small hole in the top) and let it rest overnight (at least 8 hours).

When you're ready to bake your bread, place your mini Dutch oven (with the lid on) in the oven. Preheat the oven to 450°F.

Carefully remove the very hot lid from the Dutch oven, drape a piece of parchment over the surface, and then pour your dough on top. The dough will push the parchment paper into the Dutch oven.

Place the lid back on the pan and cook for 35 minutes.

After 35 minutes, remove the lid and bake for another 15 minutes.

Let the bread cool in the Dutch oven for at least 10 minutes before moving it to a wire rack.

Slice the bread when it's cool and serve.

CHAPTER 9.
A FEW DESSERTS
FOR TWO

As my first love is scaling down dessert recipes to make smaller portions (both so we don't overeat dessert and so that I can make a new dessert everyday), I couldn't leave you without a few small-batch desserts for two.

These are the basic desserts that will spice up any date-night dinner at home.

You'll notice I use a standard 9-by-5-inch loaf pan for my desserts quite frequently. My hope is that you already have one in your cabinet, and you'll be as excited as I am to make two brownies in it, a small key lime pie, and more. You'll also need a small 6-inch cake pan to make my mini cakes for two; they're easily found at the craft store because many wedding cake bakers use this as the top layer of a wedding cake.

Cheesecake Bars with 5-Minute Microwave Lemon Curd

If I'm known for any of my desserts, it's cheesecake. It's the dessert I make most often because almost everyone loves it and so many people are afraid to make it themselves.

My cheesecake recipes always bake up perfectly flat without cracks. I can guarantee it! The reason is that I don't call for many eggs in my recipe, and I also recommend not beating too much air into the mixture.

Try these cheesecake bars made in a loaf pan the next time your cheesecake craving hits. The microwave lemon curd is just the icing on the, well, cheesecake.

Save the leftover egg white from the cheesecake to make the Angel Food Cake on page 285. They store perfectly in the freezer, and once you have seven egg whites, you can bake. Alternatively, add it to the pan when you're making scrambled eggs the next morning.

Makes 8 small bites of cheesecake

FOR THE CRUST

6 whole graham cracker sheets

2½ tablespoons unsalted butter, melted

1 tablespoon granulated sugar

FOR THE CHEESECAKE

One 8-ounce package cream cheese, at room temperature

¼ cup granulated sugar

1 large egg yolk

½ teaspoon vanilla extract

½ teaspoon fresh lemon juice

First, make the cheesecake bars: Lower an oven rack to the lower third position and preheat the oven to 325°F.

Line a 9-by-5-inch loaf pan with parchment paper; let the parchment paper overhang the sides to use as handles to lift out the cheesecake once it's baked. Set it aside.

In the bowl of a food processor (or a plastic bag), crush the graham crackers into crumbs. Stir the melted butter and granulated sugar into the graham cracker crumbs.

Push the mixture firmly into the prepared pan.

Bake for 20 to 22 minutes, until it's crisp and beginning to turn light brown.

(continued)

FOR THE LEMON CURD

⅓ cup granulated sugar

1 large egg

⅓ cup freshly squeezed lemon juice

Zest of 1 lemon (about 1 teaspoon)

3 tablespoons unsalted butter, melted

Pinch of salt

Meanwhile, beat together the cream cheese and the sugar until it's light and fluffy. Beat in the egg yolk, followed by the vanilla and lemon juice.

Pour the cheesecake mixture over the crust.

Lower the oven to 300°F and bake the cheesecake for 20 to 30 minutes, until the entire surface is set and not sticky. It will have a slightly golden yellow hue. A toothpick inserted should not come out with wet batter.

Let the cheesecake cool near the oven (drastic temperature changes cause cracks in cheesecake). Once it's fully cooled, move it to the refrigerator for at least 4 hours.

While the cheesecake cools, make the lemon curd: In a microwave-safe bowl, whisk together all of the ingredients very well.

Microwave on high for 1 minute. Stop, stir, and then microwave another minute.

Stir the lemon curd, then place it back in the microwave for a final 30 seconds.

After 2 minutes and 30 seconds, begin testing the lemon curd by quickly dipping a spoon into it and running your finger over the spoon. If the line holds, the lemon curd is done. If the curd runs and fills the line you just made, try another 30 seconds in the microwave and test again. The curd will thicken considerably as it cools.

Strain the curd through a fine-mesh strainer into a jar with a lid or a small bowl (cover with plastic wrap directly on the surface of the curd if you're using this method).

Place the curd in the fridge and use it within 7 days.

To serve, slice the cheesecake into equal pieces and top with the lemon curd.

Mini Vanilla Cake

You're going to need a mini 6-inch cake pan with 2-inch sides to make this recipe, but I can nearly promise you that it will be worth it after one bite. Knowing how to make a mini cake is perfect for small celebrations at home. Add sprinkles and it can be a personal birthday cake.

The options are endless, and the buttercream roses are entirely optional!

(continued)

FOR THE CAKE

Nonstick cooking spray

6 tablespoons unsalted butter, softened

½ cup granulated sugar

1 large egg

1 tablespoon vanilla extract

¾ cup all-purpose flour

⅛ teaspoon fine salt

¼ teaspoon baking soda

6 tablespoons buttermilk (see Note)

Preheat the oven to 350°F and spray a 6-inch round cake pan with 2-inch sides with cooking spray. Line the bottom of the pan with a round of parchment paper.

In a medium bowl, beat together the butter and sugar with an electric mixer. Beat very well, about 1 to 2 minutes.

Add the egg and vanilla, and beat until they're well combined, about 15 seconds.

In a small bowl, whisk together the flour, salt, and baking soda. Add half of this mixture to the batter and beat for just a few seconds before adding half of the buttermilk. Continue beating the batter. Add the remaining dry ingredients and beat, then add the remaining buttermilk.

Scrape the batter into the prepared pan, smooth out the top, and bake on a small sheet pan for 37 to 39 minutes, until a cake tester comes out clean.

Let the cake cool on a wire rack in the pan. Then run a knife around the edge of the pan and gently tilt the cake out of the pan. Pull away the parchment paper. At this point, you can tightly wrap it in plastic wrap and freeze it for up to 2 months. Let it defrost overnight in the fridge before letting it come to room temperature on the counter. Frost the cake after it has fully defrosted.

NOTE: If you don't have buttermilk on hand or don't want to buy a whole container for just 6 tablespoons, you can make it by combining 6 tablespoons of whole milk with ½ teaspoon of apple cider vinegar. Whisk the two together and let rest for 5 minutes before using.

FOR THE VANILLA BUTTERCREAM

8 tablespoons (1 stick) unsalted
   butter, at room temperature

2 cups powdered sugar

2 teaspoons vanilla extract

1 tablespoon heavy cream

To make the buttercream, beat the butter in a medium bowl with an electric mixer until it's light and fluffy. Add the powdered sugar, vanilla, and heavy cream, and beat until it's light and fluffy again. If the mixture seems too stiff, add a splash more heavy cream.

Use a little more than half of the buttercream to frost the cake. If you made the cake ahead of time and froze it, it's best to apply a crumb coat of buttercream before applying a thick layer.

Place the remaining quarter of the buttercream in a piping bag fitted with a 1M tip and pipe roses along the outside edge of the cake. To make a rose, pipe a spiral shape: Starting at a center point, pipe the frosting around the center point, moving outward. This is entirely optional but so easy and pretty!

Mini Chocolate Cake

You can't have one without the other! I like to frost this cake with ganache while it's still in the pan, and then refrigerate it until it's firm. If you're looking for a chocolate buttercream recipe, though, use the recipe from the mini vanilla cake and add ⅓ cup of unsweetened Dutch-processed cocoa powder and an extra splash of cream.

½ cup all-purpose flour

5 tablespoons unsweetened cocoa powder

½ teaspoon baking soda

⅓ cup neutral oil

½ cup granulated sugar

⅓ cup full-fat sour cream

1 large egg

½ teaspoon vanilla extract

1 tablespoon warm coffee

FOR THE GANACHE

3 ounces semisweet chocolate, chopped

¼ cup heavy cream

Splash of light corn syrup (optional, to keep the frosting super smooth)

Preheat the oven to 350°F and spray a 6-inch round cake pan with 2-inch sides with cooking spray. Line the bottom of the pan with a round of parchment paper.

In a medium bowl, whisk together the flour, cocoa powder, and baking soda. Set aside.

In a small bowl, whisk together the oil, sugar, sour cream, egg, vanilla, and coffee.

Combine the two bowls, mixing just until they're combined.

Pour the batter into the cake pan and bake for 29 to 32 minutes, or until a toothpick inserted into the cake comes out clean. If you underbake the cake, it will sink slightly. It will also start to pull away from the sides when it's done.

Let the cake cool on a wire rack in the pan. Then turn a knife around the edge of the pan and gently tilt the cake out of the pan. Pull away the parchment paper.

Next, make the ganache frosting: In a double boiler or a metal bowl fitted over a pan of simmering water, combine the chopped chocolate, cream, and corn syrup (if using). Stir it over medium heat until it's melted and smooth. Alternatively, you can melt the chocolate and cream in the microwave in 25-second pulses on low power. Stir between each pulse.

Pour the chocolate over the cake and refrigerate it until it's set, about 20 minutes. Serve at room temperature.

Angel Food Cake in a Loaf Pan

Angel food cake is one of my favorite cakes of all time. It's light, airy, and just faintly sweet. The sugar crust on the top is my absolute favorite, and when it's baked in a loaf pan you get plenty of it.

While this recipe serves slightly more than two people, since you'll get seven or eight slices, it's significantly less than a standard angel food cake recipe. You only need seven egg whites for this recipe. The microwave lemon curd on page 278 is great drizzled on top, too!

¾ cup granulated sugar, divided

½ cup all-purpose flour

1 tablespoon cornstarch

7 large egg whites

2 teaspoons vanilla extract

¾ teaspoon cream of tartar (optional, see Note)

¼ teaspoon fine sea salt

Whipped cream, for garnish

Fresh raspberries, for garnish

Preheat the oven to 325°F and have a 9-by-5-inch loaf pan ready. Ensure it is not nonstick. Do not line or grease the pan in any way. Trust me!

In a small bowl, whisk together ¼ cup of the sugar, the flour, and the cornstarch. Set aside.

Add the egg whites, vanilla, cream of tartar (if using), and salt to the bowl of a mini stand mixer. Beat the mixture on medium until it's foamy, about 30 seconds. Slowly stream in the remaining ½ cup of granulated sugar, 1 tablespoon at a time, while the mixer runs. Continue to beat on high speed until soft, floppy peaks form, about 4 minutes.

Next, add one-third of the dry ingredients and gently fold them into the egg whites using a rubber spatula. Proper folding technique is down the middle and around the sides. Your goal is to incorporate the flour mixture without deflating the air you just whipped into the egg whites.

Repeat with the remaining flour mixture in two increments. Take your time; it will take at least 5 minutes to fold everything together gently. Be sure no lumps of flour remain (or they will rise to the surface of your cake while baking).

(continued)

Pour the batter into the loaf pan. Place the loaf pan on a baking sheet and bake for 38 to 42 minutes. The cake is done when the top is no longer sticky to the touch, and if it cracks the cracks won't be sticky either.

Once the cake comes out of the oven, immediately turn it upside down and invert it over two cans. The cake needs to cool upside down so it doesn't deflate. Let it cool for at least 60 minutes.

Once the cake is cool, run a knife around the edges of the pan and gently let the cake fall onto a cutting board on its side.

Use a serrated knife to slice the cake into even slices. Go slow and don't smush the cake while slicing.

Serve with whipped cream and raspberries.

NOTE: If you don't have cream of tartar, leave it out. The cake won't rise as high, but it will still taste great!

Raspberry Brownies with Chambord Glaze

If I'm picking a Valentine's Day dessert, it's going to be brownies. My brownies are baked in a loaf pan, and when cut down the middle after baking they make two perfectly portioned brownies. My brownies have an intense chocolate hit from unsweetened cocoa powder, plus a small amount of flour for chewiness.

Unlike cake batters that you must gently fold together, I ask you to beat the heck out of the batter before spreading it in the pan. Roll your sleeves up, get in there, and activate that gluten in the flour! Fifty rough strokes! Gluten is what gives brownies their chew. It's so worth it!

Dollop raspberries on top of the batter before baking and drizzle these with a Chambord (raspberry liquor) glaze for the best chocolate raspberry dessert you've ever had.

FOR THE BROWNIES

5 tablespoons (2½ ounces) unsalted butter

½ cup plus 2 tablespoons granulated sugar

½ cup unsweetened cocoa powder

½ teaspoon vanilla extract

¼ teaspoon almond extract

¼ teaspoon salt

1 large egg

¼ cup all-purpose flour

Small handful fresh raspberries

FOR THE CHAMBORD GLAZE

½ cup powdered sugar

1 tablespoon Chambord (raspberry liqueur)

Preheat the oven to 325°F and make sure an oven rack is in the lower third of the oven.

Line a 9-by-5-inch loaf pan with parchment paper in two directions, overlapping; let the parchment paper overhang the sides to use as handles to lift out the brownies once they're baked.

Next, in a microwave-safe bowl, combine the butter, sugar, and cocoa powder.

Microwave for 30 seconds, stop and stir, and microwave for another 30 seconds. The mixture will be quite hot. (If you do not have a microwave, add everything to a small saucepan over low heat and cook while stirring until everything melts and begins to bubble. Turn the heat off and remove the pan from the stove. Then proceed with the recipe).

Let the mixture rest on the counter for a few minutes to cool, stirring occasionally.

When the mixture feels warm but not hot, stir in the vanilla, almond extract, and salt. Finally, stir in the egg.

(continued)

Add the flour to the batter and, using a spatula, vigorously stir the mixture for 50 strokes. This activates the gluten and makes for rich, chewy brownies.

Spread the batter evenly into the prepared pan. Sprinkle the raspberries on top, pressing some into the batter.

Bake for 23 to 26 minutes, until the top is dry.

While the brownies cool, whisk together the glaze in a small bowl. Add more Chambord as needed to make a smooth glaze.

Drizzle the glaze over the brownies, cut them into pieces, and serve.

Key Lime Pie in a Loaf Pan

My love for key lime pie does not have a limit—in other words, if you put an entire key lime pie in front of me, I will eat the whole pie. So, I scaled down my favorite recipe for key lime pie (a simple recipe, really) and bake it in a 9-by-5-inch loaf pan.

The only real trick here is to use a shot glass to force the graham cracker crumbs up the sides of the pan so that they hold all of the pie filling.

Note that I've used regular limes in this recipe, but also call for 1 tablespoon of fresh lemon juice to mimic the flavors of a true key lime. However, if you have real key limes, please use them! You need ¼ cup of citrus juice in total.

Makes 5 small slices of pie

FOR THE CRUST

Nonstick cooking spray

8 whole graham cracker sheets

3 tablespoons (1½ ounces) unsalted butter, melted

1½ tablespoons granulated sugar

FOR THE FILLING

One 14-ounce can sweetened condensed milk

Juice and zest of 3 limes (3 tablespoons total juice), plus extra zest for serving

1 tablespoon fresh lemon juice

3 large egg yolks

Freshly whipped cream, for serving

Preheat the oven to 350°F.

Line a 9-by-5-inch loaf pan with parchment paper; let the parchment paper overhang the sides to use as handles to lift out the pie once it's baked. Spray the pan with cooking spray.

In a food processor, combine the graham crackers, melted butter, and sugar. Pulse until the crumbs are fine and look like wet sand.

Press the graham cracker crumbs into the pan, and, using a shot glass, press the crust up all sides of the pan by 1 inch. Take your time and press it firmly.

Bake the crust for 10 minutes, then remove it from the oven and let cool. Leave the oven on.

Meanwhile, in a small bowl, whisk together the condensed milk, citrus juices, and egg yolks (reserve the egg whites for another use). Using a microplane grater, grate the zest of 1 lime into the mixture and whisk to combine.

Pour the filling into the crust and slide it back into the oven for 18 to 20 minutes. When the pie is done, it will be slightly jiggly.

(continued)

Let the pie cool to room temperature, cover it with plastic wrap loosely, and refrigerate it overnight.

When you're ready to serve it, use the parchment paper handles to gently lift out the pie. Slice it into five pieces and serve with whipped cream and extra freshly grated lime zest on top.

Two Mini Apple Pies

I love using mini 6-inch pie dishes to make personal pies. Sometimes sharing a dessert is romantic, and sometimes I just want to eat the whole pie by myself—which I can, if it's mini!

The type of apples you use in an apple pie always matters, but it matters a bit more with a small pie. Here's why: since we're baking mini pies with a lesser amount of crust that browns faster in the oven, we really have to make sure the apples are going to soften in our 30-minute bake time. For this reason, I recommend a mix of Golden Delicious and Braeburn apples. These apples will soften and release their juices in the time it takes for the mini pie to bake.

Makes 2 (6-inch) pies

FOR THE CRUST

2 ounces of shortening, cold

12 tablespoons unsalted butter, cold

2½ cups all-purpose flour, plus extra for rolling

1¼ teaspoon salt

FOR THE APPLE FILLING

6 small apples (preferably mix of Golden Delicious and Braeburn)

¼ cup granulated sugar

2 tablespoons all-purpose flour

Juice and zest of ½ lemon

½ teaspoon cinnamon

¼ teaspoon ground allspice

¼ teaspoon ground cloves

1 tablespoon unsalted butter

1 large egg yolk, beaten

Coarse sugar, for sprinkling on top (optional)

First, make the crust: Dice the shortening and butter into ½-inch cubes and place them on a plate in the freezer for about 15 minutes.

In a large bowl, combine the flour and the salt, and whisk them lightly to combine.

Add the chilled shortening and butter to the flour mixture. Use two forks or a pastry blender to combine. Incorporate the fats into the flour until the pieces are slightly smaller than peas. Don't overmix.

Evenly drizzle ½ cup ice water over the mixture in two batches, stirring gently to combine. The dough should start to clump together (but not seem overly wet), and there should be no dry patches of flour.

Scrape the dough into a large ball, flatten it into a disk, wrap it in plastic wrap, and refrigerate it for at least 2 hours.

When the dough only has about 30 minutes of refrigeration time left, peel, core, and slice the apples into ¼-inch slices.

Place the sliced apples in a bowl and stir in the sugar, flour, lemon zest, lemon juice, and all of

(continued)

the spices. Set them aside to rest while you roll out the dough.

After the dough has chilled for 2 hours, lightly dust your counter with flour. Divide the dough into four pieces, leaving two slightly larger than the other two (these will be the bottom crusts).

Preheat the oven to 375°F.

Roll out the two larger pieces of dough to about 9 inches in diameter to fit inside the 6-inch pie pans. Drape the bottom crust in the pie plate, leaving plenty draping over the edges for crimping and sealing, and set it aside. Next, roll out the two smaller pieces of dough to about 8 inches in diameter, and, using a pizza wheel, cut 10 to 11 strips of dough that are 1 inch wide.

If you want to make a plain lattice, leave the dough strips as is. If you'd like to braid the dough, cut three thin pieces of dough from the 1-inch strips. If you want to alternate thin and thick pieces of dough, make the thin ones by cutting the 1-inch strips in half.

When you're ready to lattice the top of the pies, pour the apples into the pie pans. Pack the apples in very tightly. Be sure to include the accumulated juices in the bottom of the bowl.

Dice the remaining tablespoon of butter and spread it evenly on top of the apples.

Drape the strips of dough on top of the apples in one direction. To make a lattice, alternate flipping pieces back to weave in a strip of dough in the opposite direction.

Once the tops of the pies are latticed, trim the excess dough from the edges and pinch the bottom and top piecrusts together. Use your fingers to crimp around the edges to seal in the apples completely.

Finally, beat the egg yolk with a splash of water and brush it over the surface of the piecrust.

Sprinkle coarse sugar on top of the pies. Place the pies on a baking sheet and slide into the oven.

Bake them for about 30 minutes, checking to see if the crust is browning too much at around 20 to 25 minutes. If so, cover it loosely with foil to shield it from the heat of the oven.

After 30 minutes of baking, use a knife to poke some apples and see if they're done. The pie is done when the apples are fork-tender and the filling is bubbling, about 30 to 40 minutes (use a foil shield as much as you need to).

Let the pies cool completely before attempting to slice and serve.

Mini Chocolate Cream Pie

This is the recipe that launched my career in food. After tasting my family's recipe for chocolate cream pie and hearing the story about how my grandpa missed this pie so much when he was serving in Pearl Harbor that he ate an entire pan of it upon his homecoming, I knew I had to share the recipe. It was actually the first recipe I ever shared on my blog back in 2010 and I never dreamed it would be the start of my career in food. After one bite, you'll have a hard time deciding if this serves one or two!

Makes 1 (6-inch) pie

FOR THE CRUST

4 whole graham cracker sheets

2½ tablespoons unsalted butter, melted

Pinch of cinnamon

2 teaspoons sugar

FOR THE FILLING

¼ cup sugar

3 tablespoons unsweetened cocoa powder

2½ tablespoons cornstarch

1½ cups milk (I've used 1% and 2% successfully)

1 large egg yolk

1 teaspoon vanilla extract

1 tablespoon butter

FOR THE WHIPPED CREAM

4 tablespoons heavy whipping cream

2 tablespoons powdered sugar

¼ teaspoon vanilla extract

Preheat the oven to 350°F.

Pulse the graham crackers, melted butter, cinnamon, and sugar in a food processor. Alternatively, you can crush them in a plastic storage bag. Make sure the crumbs are very fine. Press the mixture into the pie tin, using the bottom of a glass or small measuring cup to pack the crumbs firmly. Press the crust up the edges of the pie tin.

Bake the crust on a cookie sheet for 10 minutes. Remove it from the oven and let it cool while you make the chocolate filling.

Sift the sugar, cocoa powder, and cornstarch into a small bowl. Add ½ cup of the milk and whisk vigorously until the mixture is very smooth and free of lumps. Slowly add the rest of the milk while whisking constantly. Finally, whisk in the egg yolk.

Pour the mixture into a small pan and bring it to a simmer over medium heat. Stir the mixture constantly with a wooden spoon, being sure to scrape the corners of the pan with the spoon. Once the mixture starts to thicken and simmer, turn the heat to low and continue cooking for 1 minute. The mixture should be silky and slightly thickened—it will firm up in the crust later. To test the thickness, coat the back of a spoon with

the mixture and quickly run your finger through it. If the pudding holds the line, you're good! If it runs back together, it still needs a few minutes of cooking.

Remove the pan from the heat and add the butter. Stir to melt it, then stir in the vanilla. Pour the pudding into the crust. Press plastic wrap against the surface of the pudding and chill in the fridge for at least 4 hours or overnight.

When you're ready to serve the pie, whip the heavy cream, sugar, and vanilla together until a thick whipped cream forms. Spread it evenly on top of the pie, slice, and serve.

Coconut Carrot Cake Cupcakes

I shared a recipe for carrot cake cupcakes in my first book, *Dessert for Two,* but since then I've developed a love for a carrot cake cupcake with a bit more chew (a few more chunks in the mix, if you will). While coconut flakes in carrot cake can make carrot cake purists angry, hey, at least I didn't put raisins in it, OK? P.S. I secretly love raisins in carrot cake but fear your judgment for saying so.

  The cupcakes keep for up to 3 days, refrigerated. Let them rest on the counter about 20 minutes before serving.

Makes 6 cupcakes

FOR THE CUPCAKES

½ cup plus 2 tablespoons flour (10 tablespoons total)

½ teaspoon ground cinnamon

¼ teaspoon ground cloves

¼ teaspoon freshly ground nutmeg

¼ teaspoon ground ginger

½ teaspoon baking powder

¼ teaspoon baking soda

¼ teaspoon salt

½ cup freshly grated carrot

⅓ cup sweetened coconut flakes

½ cup packed light brown sugar

1 large egg

2 tablespoons sour cream

½ teaspoon vanilla extract

¼ cup neutral oil (canola or grapeseed oil)

Preheat the oven to 350°F and line six cups in a muffin tin with paper liners.

In a large bowl, thoroughly whisk together the flour, cinnamon, cloves, nutmeg, ginger, baking powder, baking soda, and salt. Add the grated carrots and coconut, and whisk very well to combine. The flour coats the carrot and coconut pieces and prevents them from sinking to the bottom of the cupcakes.

In a separate bowl, whisk together the brown sugar, egg, sour cream, vanilla, and oil.

Combine the wet and dry ingredients, and stir until just blended.

Divide the mixture between the cupcake liners and bake for 24 to 27 minutes, or until a toothpick inserted comes out with only moist crumbs clinging to it.

Let the cupcakes cool completely while you make the frosting.

CREAM CHEESE FROSTING

Half an 8-ounce block cream
   cheese, at room temperature

3 tablespoons unsalted butter,
   at room temperature

1½ cups powdered sugar

½ teaspoon vanilla extract

Beat together the cream cheese, butter,
powdered sugar, and vanilla untilt light and fluffy.

Frost the cupcakes with a knife or piping bag
fitted with a tip.

Cookies and Cream Cupcakes

Sometimes, the best way to show your love is with a small batch of chocolate cupcakes with cookies-and-cream buttercream frosting on top.

Since I bake for a living, I don't typically allow my husband to have store-bought cookies in the house. It only seems fair that, if I always have freshly baked cookies on the counter, he probably shouldn't go to the store and *buy* cookies, right? Please take my side. I finally gave in and stopped denying my husband's love for chocolate sandwich cookies. I bought him a box (of organic, all-natural ones, hah!), and he was shocked. Then, when I made Cookies and Cream Cupcakes with them, he was even more shocked!

Makes 4 cupcakes

FOR THE CUPCAKES

⅓ cup all-purpose flour

2 tablespoons (slightly heaped) unsweetened cocoa powder

¼ teaspoon baking soda

¼ teaspoon baking powder

½ teaspoon instant espresso powder (optional)

⅓ cup buttermilk

4 teaspoons canola oil

½ teaspoon vanilla extract

¼ cup packed dark brown sugar

FOR THE FROSTING

4 tablespoons unsalted butter, softened

1 cup powdered sugar

1 tablespoon heavy cream

½ teaspoon vanilla extract

4 chocolate sandwich cookies

Preheat the oven to 350°F and line four cups in a muffin tin with paper liners.

In a medium bowl, whisk together the flour, cocoa, baking soda, baking powder, and espresso powder (if using).

Next, in a small measuring cup, thoroughly whisk together the buttermilk, oil, vanilla, and brown sugar.

Add the wet ingredients to the dry ingredients and stir until they're just mixed.

Divide the batter between the cupcake liners and bake for 16 to 17 minutes. They're done when the tops spring back when touched (if you under-bake, they'll sink). Let the cupcakes cool completely.

In a small bowl, beat together the butter, powdered sugar, heavy cream, and vanilla using an electric mixer on high. Beat the mixture for 1 minute, until it's very fluffy and light.

Finally, stir in the cookies by hand, crushing them as you add them. (I went a little light on the cookies so the frosting was more photogenic, but the frosting tastes best when you add all four cookies).

Frost the cooled cupcakes and serve.

5-Minute Chocolate Mousse

I make this easy chocolate mousse every single year for Valentine's Day dessert. Even if we have dessert at a restaurant, we come home to two small pots of this chocolate mousse. It seems fancy, but it's easy enough to make any night that you have a date night at home.

   You can make it ahead of time and store it in the fridge, but let it sit for about 20 minutes at room temperature before serving. The chocolate will harden in the fridge, so this is actually the most important step!

1 large pasteurized egg
½ cup heavy cream
1 tablespoon powdered sugar
5 ounces milk chocolate chips
   (heaping ¾ cup)
1 tablespoon unsalted butter

Separate the egg and have the egg yolk ready in a bowl nearby. Save the egg white for another use.

Pour the heavy cream in a medium bowl and place it in the fridge with the electric beaters. (We're prechilling to speed up the whipping time.)

Melt the chocolate: In a medium glass bowl, add the chocolate chips and butter. Turn the microwave power down to 50% and microwave for 20 seconds. Stop microwaving and stir. Repeat until about ⅔ of the chocolate chips are melted. For the remaining chips to melt, slowly and gently stir the mixture with a wooden spoon. The residual heat of the bowl will melt the rest. The mixture should be smooth. (If the mixture is pasty or grainy, you have burned the chocolate and you must start over.) Stir in the egg yolk.

Once the chocolate is melted, work quickly! Whip the cream in the prechilled bowl using the prechilled beaters in an electric mixer on high. Once the cream has soft peaks, add the powdered sugar and all of the melted chocolate. If the chocolate has started to firm up slightly, it's fine—just work fast.

Beat the chocolate into the cream mixture until it's fully incorporated, about 15 seconds maximum.

Divide the mousse between two serving dishes.

Serve immediately, or chill it for up to 3 days but bring it to room temperature for 20 minutes before serving (it will harden a bit in the fridge).

Strawberry Mousse

When I taste a dessert that I really like, I feel a chill on the back of my arms. This is one of those chill-inducing desserts. It tastes so light and creamy, yet the flavors are complex, if that makes sense.

   Have you ever dipped a strawberry in sour cream and then rolled it in brown sugar? That's what this reminds me of. The tang from the sour cream and cream cheese just cozies right up to the berries. Use very high-quality strawberry jam (not jelly) that tastes like the essence of freshly picked strawberries. Also, don't leave out the salt—it's critical for flavor balancing here.

½ cup strawberry jam

¼ teaspoon kosher salt

⅓ cup sour cream

3 ounces cream cheese

⅓ cup heavy cream

1 tablespoon powdered sugar

1 teaspoon rose water
   (optional)

Place the jam, salt, sour cream, and cream cheese in a blender (or food processor). Puree the mixture until it's smooth.

In a separate bowl, add the heavy cream and whip until soft peaks form. Add the powdered sugar and beat to combine.

Fold the two mixtures together and stir in the rose water.

Divide the mousse between two serving bowls and chill them for 1 hour before serving.

Chocolate Fondue for Two

If you pulled out your fondue pot to make my Classic Cheese Fondue for Two on page 172, keep it out to make this chocolate version!

⅓ cup half-and-half
5 ounces chocolate (chips or chopped chocolate)
Fresh fruits: pineapple, bananas, and strawberries
Jumbo marshmallows
Small cookies: vanilla wafers, wafer cookies, and bite-size chocolate chip cookies
Pretzels

Heat the half-and-half in your fondue pot over high heat until it's just simmering—bubbles should be forming around the edges of the pan and steam will be rising up—but do not let it boil.

Turn off the heat and add the chocolate to the fondue pot. Let the mixture sit for 1 minute before gently stirring it together. At first it won't look like it will come together, but it will! Keep stirring until it's smooth and creamy.

Serve with fresh fruit, marshmallows, cookies, and pretzels. Enjoy!

S'mores Baked Alaska

I love using a muffin pan to make individual desserts. This S'mores Baked Alaska is easy: line a few muffin cups with crushed graham crackers, smush your favorite chocolate ice cream on top, and store it in the freezer until you're ready.

   The day of, make the marshmallow fluff. When you're ready (and you really know you're ready), remove the ice cream pucks from the muffin pan, place them on a serving plate, cover them with the marshmallow fluff, and torch! Yes, the torch is going to slightly melt the ice cream. It's okay. It's life. And it's delicious.

Makes 4 Alaskas

4 whole graham cracker sheets

1½ tablespoons unsalted
   butter, melted

1 pint chocolate ice cream

2½ cups sugar

½ cup light corn syrup

2 large egg whites

¼ teaspoon cream of tartar

NOTE: You can torch these in the oven using the broiler setting, but keep an eye on them—they brown quickly.

Line four muffin cups in a pan with plastic wrap, overlapping as necessary.

Crush the graham crackers into crumbs using a plastic bag or a food processor. You should get about ½ cup of crumbs.

Combine the graham cracker crumbs and the melted butter in a small bowl. Press the crumbs into each muffin cup firmly. Place the pan in the freezer for 30 minutes.

Meanwhile, soften the chocolate ice cream until it's easy to scoop.

Remove the pan from the freezer and smush chocolate ice cream into each of the cups, leveling the surface so that it's flat. Return the pan to the freezer for at least 4 hours, or up to 2 days in advance.

On serving day, make the marshmallow fluff: In a small saucepan, combine the 3 tablespoons water, the sugar, and corn syrup. Stir together gently (try not to splash sugar crystals on the edges of the pan).

Turn the heat to medium-high and bring the mixture to 240°F.

Meanwhile, add the egg whites and the cream of tartar to the bowl of a stand mixer. Beat them until soft peaks form, about 3 to 4 minutes.

When the sugar syrup mixture reaches 240°F, immediately remove it from the heat and stream it into the egg whites while mixing on high speed.

Beat on high speed until light and fluffy, about 4 to 5 minutes. Let the marshmallow fluff cool completely (about 4 to 5 hours before serving).

When you want to serve, remove each ice cream puck from the muffin pan and place it on a serving plate and spread with fluff. You can freeze these covered in fluff up to 4 hours, too.

Use a culinary torch to lightly toast the fluff. Serve immediately.

Small-Batch Espresso Chocolate Chip Cookies

In our search for a chocolate chip cookie "house recipe," we've been through a lot of butter and chocolate chips. Who says marriage is hard work? We've got cookies! This recipe is nearly a decade in the making, and it's finally perfect. I add an indecent amount of espresso powder and a heavy pinch of salt. They're addicting!

Makes 1 dozen small cookies

6 tablespoons salted butter

¼ cup dark brown sugar

3 tablespoons granulated sugar

1 large egg yolk

½ vanilla bean, sliced open and scraped

½ cup plus 2 tablespoons all-purpose flour

¼ teaspoon fine sea salt

1 heaping teaspoon instant espresso powder

¼ teaspoon baking soda

¼ teaspoon baking powder

⅓ cup semisweet chocolate chips

Preheat the oven to 375°F. Line a light-colored baking sheet with a silicone mat.

In a medium bowl, beat the butter with an electric mixer on medium speed until it's fluffy, about 20 seconds.

Add the sugars and beat for another 30 seconds. The mixture will turn a pale color and be fluffy.

Next, add the egg yolk and the insides from the vanilla bean and beat until they're just combined.

Whisk together the flour, salt, espresso powder, baking soda, and baking powder in a separate bowl.

Sprinkle the flour mixture on top of the butter mixture and beat just until they're combined.

Stir in the chocolate chips.

Scoop the dough into 12 dough balls and space them evenly on the baking sheet.

Bake for 8 to 10 minutes, removing the cookies from the oven when the edges just start to turn golden brown.

Let the cookies rest on the baking sheet for 1 minute before moving them to a wire rack to cool.

LEFTOVERS

What to do with half a can of this or that/the remaining portion of fresh herbs/ the rest of the container? Because leftovers can often lead to food waste, I compiled a list of recipes that help you use the rest of the can of tomatoes, the remaining portions of beans, fresh herbs, cheese blocks, and even condiments!

Recipes that use CANNED TOMATOES:

Spaghetti with Small-Batch Meat Sauce (page 32)
Mexican Quinoa with Avocado (page 66)
Baked Greek Shrimp (page 84)
Sloppy Joe Tater Tot Skillet (page 90)
Tortilla Soup (page 104)
Minestrone/Ribollita (page 106)
Black Bean Lasagna Bowls (page 114)
Smoky Pork and Yellow Rice Paella Bowls (page 132)
Pizza Baguettes (page 207)
Quick and Easy Pizza Sauce (page 209)
Barbecue Chicken Cornbread Casserole (page 221)

Recipes that use SUN-DRIED TOMATOES:

Spinach Pesto Pasta with Walnuts (page 34)
Creamy Mushroom Chicken Skillet (page 88)
Chicken Sausage with Orzo and Broccolini (page 94)

Recipes that use CHERRY TOMATOES:

One-Pot Crispy Salami and Cherry Tomato Pasta (page 62)
Summertime Chilaquiles (page 72)

Recipes that use GROUND MEAT:

Beef

Turkey

Recipes that use FRESH HERBS:

Cilantro

Recipes that use CHEESE:

Bourbon-Glazed Turkey Burgers (Gruyère) (page 204)

Pizza Baguettes (mozzarella) (page 207)

Creamy Chicken Enchiladas (pepper Jack) (page 218)

Barbecue Chicken Cornbread Casserole (Cheddar) (page 221)

Engagement Chicken Pasta (cream cheese) (page 224)

Loaded Potato Soup (Cheddar) (page 228)

Master Cheese Sauce (Cheddar) (page 233)

Broccoli Cheese Soup (Cheddar) (page 234)

Totchos (Cheddar) (page 237)

Green Chile Mac & Cheese (Cheddar) (page 238)

Veggie Hash Over Pasta (mascarpone) (page 252)

Cacio e Pepe Polenta Casserole (mozzarella) (page 255)

Cheddar Garlic Biscuits (page 268)

Recipes that use BUTTERMILK:

Cheddar Scallion Waffles (page 196)

Jalapeño Cornbread Muffins (page 267)

Cheddar Garlic Biscuits (page 268)

Mini Vanilla Cake (page 279)

Recipes that use BEANS:

Mexican Quinoa with Avocado (black beans) (page 66)

Summertime Chilaquiles (black beans) (page 72)

French Lentils and Kielbasa (page 80)

Minestrone/Ribollita (kidney beans) (page 106)

Black Bean Lasagna Bowls (page 114)

Chicken Burrito Bowls (black beans) (page 130)

Lentil Enchiladas (page 157)

Best-Ever Veggie Sandwiches (black beans) (page 195)

Creamy Chicken Enchiladas (cranberry beans or Great Northern white beans)
   (page 218)

Southwestern Chicken Cobb Salad (black beans) (page 222)

Recipes that use PRODUCE:

Melting Sweet Potatoes (page 189)

Roasted Veggies (page 249)

Russet Potatoes

Zuppa Toscana (page 111)

Oven Fries for Special Times (page 186)

Really Good Mashed Potatoes (page 227)

Loaded Potato Soup (page 228)

Samosa Potato Patties (page 231)

Roasted Veggies (page 249)

Yukon Golds

Steak for Two with Scalloped Potatoes (page 74)

Roasted Potato Bowls with Broccoli and Gribiche (page 134)

Classic Cheese Fondue for Two (page 172)

Onions and Garlic

Almost every recipe in the book calls for onions, garlic, or some member of the allium family. If you're looking for a way to use up a lot of onions, try making Pressure Cooker Caramelized Onions (page 46) and storing them in the freezer for later meals.

Recipes that use EGGS:

Mini Quiche Lorraine with Salad (and the Only Salad Dressing You'll Ever Need) (page 160)

Roasted Potato Bowls with Broccoli and Gribiche (page 134)

Cheddar Scallion Waffles (page 196)

Veggie Hash Under Eggs (page 251)

Brioche-Style Hamburger Buns (page 260)

Perfect Dinner Rolls (page 264)

Jalapeño Corn Muffins (page 267)

Recipes that use SOUR CREAM/YOGURT:

Mexican Quinoa with Avocado (page 66)

Mexican Street Corn Tacos (page 70)

Black Bean Lasagna Bowls (page 114)

Creamy Chicken Enchiladas (page 218)

Southwestern Chicken Cobb Salad (page 222)

Totchos (page 237)

Recipes that use CONDIMENTS:

Mayonnaise

Mexican Street Corn Tacos (page 70)

Chicken Burrito Bowls (page 130)

Best-Ever Bean Burgers (page 244)

Mustard

Cheesy Broccoli Quinoa (mustard powder) (page 65)

French Lentils and Kielbasa (Dijon) (page 80)

Sloppy Joe Tater Tot Skillet (yellow) (page 90)

Roasted Potato Bowls with Broccoli and Gribiche (Dijon) (page 134)

Classic Cheese Fondue for Two (Dijon) (page 172)

Southwestern Chicken Cobb Salad (Dijon) (page 222)

Broccoli Cheese Soup (mustard powder) (page 234)

Recipes that use VINEGAR:

Rice Wine Vinegar

Chicken Lettuce Cups (page 69)

Almost Korean Beef Bowls (page 116)

Coconut Curry Noodle Bowls (page 126)

Crunchiest Chinese Chicken Salad (page 136)

Carrot Ginger Salmon (page 153)

Thai Peanut Roast Beef Wraps (page 210)

Recipes that use FROZEN VEGGIES:

Recipes that use GRAINS:

ACKNOWLEDGMENTS

Sincerest and deepest THANK YOU to my family and friends who continue to support this crazy life I've chosen. I promise to reward you with many small batches of cookies and dinners for my entire life . . . if I could just get one more night of free babysitting, please? :)

In many ways, this book felt like my life's work—my only chance to convince the world how essential small-batch cooking can be. It's hard to convey your life's deepest passion without facing a hefty amount of self-doubt.

Many, many thanks to my colleagues who fielded my worries with compassion and confidence. Heidi Swanson, you are a gem. Joy Wilson, you're my role model and a statue of calm confidence and grace. Thank you, Emily Stoffel and Sarah Menanix—our "Mama Tribe" keeps me sane and safe (and nodding emphatically). Sherrie Castellano, you're my better half. Amber Bracegirdle, my love for you is as big as Texas.

And thank you to every other woman in my life, especially Esther Hall, who motivates me to choose the positive path when I so desperately want to travel the negative one. May we continue to lean on each other, raise each other up, and also press on together.

Thank you to my publisher for sorting through my body of recipes and turning them into something that will inspire couples to cook together and grow in love. The work that you do which encourages such things is everlasting.

Unending, eternal gratitude to God for giving me a spark of passion that fuels me right out of bed in the morning and far into the late-night hours, and to Jesus for showing me how to live while pursuing it.

INDEX